The late LEONARD SILK was economics columnist of the *New York Times* and Chairman of the Editorial Board of *Business Week*. His many books include *The Research Revolution, Economics in Plain English, Economics in the Real World,* and *Nixonomics.*

MARK SILK is Director of the Center for the Study of Religion in Public Life at Trinity College in Hartford, Connecticut. Formerly with the *Atlanta Journal-Constitution,* he is the author of *Spiritual Politics: Religion in America Since World War II* and *Unsecular Media: Making News of Religion in America.*

Making Capitalism Work

MAKING CAPITALISM WORK

Leonard Silk and Mark Silk

with Robert Heilbroner, Jonas Pontusson,
and Bernard Wasow

A TWENTIETH CENTURY FUND BOOK

New York University Press · New York and London

New York University Press
New York and London
Copyright © 1996 Twentieth Century Fund

The Twentieth Century Fund sponsors and supervises timely analyses of economic policy, foreign affairs, and domestic political issues. Not-for-profit and nonpartisan, the Fund was founded in 1919 and endowed by Edward A. Filene.

Library of Congress Cataloging-in-Publication Data
Silk, Leonard Solomon, 1918-
Making capitalism work / Leonard Silk and Mark Silk ; with Robert Heilbroner, Jonas Pontusson, and Bernard Wasow.
p.   cm.
"A Twentieth Century Fund book."
Includes bibliographical reference and index.
ISBN 0-8147-8064-4 (alk. paper)
1. Capitalism. 2. Post-communism. 3. Economic policy. I. Silk, Mark. II. Title.
HB501.S5896   1996
330.12'2—dc20   96-25257
CIP

New York University Press books are printed on acid-free paper, and their binding materials are chosen for strength and durability.

Manufactured in the United States of America

10 9 8 7 6 5 4 3 2 1

The passions that incline man to peace, are fear of death; desire of such things as are necessary to commodious living; and a hope by their industry to attain them. And reason suggesteth convenient articles of peace, upon which men may be drawn to agreement.

—Thomas Hobbes

CONTENTS

···

Economics in Plain English, and *The Economists.* His long and distinguished career was characterized by an insistence on understanding and explaining the reality of economics—of looking at the facts to see what was actually happening to people and institutions.

Leonard Silk believed that economists, rather than merely cataloging global economic developments as the best of all possible world market outcomes, had a special obligation to develop ideas and offer policy options that could change the path of the economy. An advocate of full employment policies and substantial investment in education, infrastructure, and alleviation of social ills, he sought answers in the rapidly changing pattern of economic activity in other countries, as well as our own.

Beginning in 1992, Silk began a conversation with the Fund about a book that would address the changing global topology of capitalism. He was excited by the wide variety of experiments under way in nations that previously had been neither democratic nor capitalist. He also felt that insufficient attention had been paid to the lessons offered by the Western European countries and Japan, with their highly individualist adaptations to mixed capitalism. And, he was particularly disappointed in the current role of most American economists in the national and international discussions about what was occurring and what should and should not be done to deal with it. He also was alarmed by many of the current trends in American economic performance. He noted, for example, that the percentage of unemployed who stay unemployed six months or more increased from 5 percent in 1970 to more than 20 percent in 1992. He discussed the import of a survey that indicated that virtually every Fortune 500 CEO planned to downsize. All this and more became rich material for his book-in-progress.

It was a book that Silk would never finish. Diagnosed with a serious form of cancer, he fought back, both against the disease itself and against the curtailment of his project. As the illness took an ever more aggressive course, Leonard Silk's determination to find a way to complete what would be his last book only increased. His struggle was difficult but, in the most important sense, he triumphed.

Since its inception more than seventy-five years ago, the Fund has supported many works that respond to our founding idea, that markets and government must be judged by their contributions to the well-being of all citizens. Our recent output in this area includes Edward Wolff's *Top Heavy: A Study of the Increasing Inequality of Wealth in America* and *The Report of a Task Force on Market Speculation and Corporate Governance*, with a background paper, "Who's Minding the Store?" by Robert Shiller. This year, Robert Kuttner's important book for the Fund, *Everything for Sale*, exploring the virtues and limits of markets, will be published. And we are currently supporting a study of public policy and economic growth by Barry Bluestone and Bennett Harrison, as well as a book on the causes of income inequality by James Galbraith. We hope that Leonard Silk's book will be seen as one of the centerpieces in this current group of Fund publications focused on political economy.

On behalf of the Fund's trustees, I thank Leonard Silk's son, Mark, who by taking on what became the role of co-author, preserved the heart of his father's ideas and the thrust of his writing. He built upon the draft material to bring his father's vision of this book to life. We also are especially appreciative of the chapters contributed by Robert Heilbroner, Jonas Pontusson, and Bernard Wasow. These distinguished scholars of economic affairs enriched this volume with their insights about capitalism in the modern world.

Finally, it is worth noting that most of us, as we grow older, seem to learn less from each new experience; rather we tend to become more narrow in our view of the world and its possibilities. Leonard Silk, on the other hand, was that rare human being about whom the opposite was true. *Making Capitalism Work* is the result of a collaborative effort, but it is also an expression of one man's determination to continue to question, explain, and make a difference. I thank Leonard Silk for working with us on this book—it was a personal honor to be graced by his friendship.

April 1996   Richard C. Leone, President
                                    The Twentieth Century Fund

Preface

Mark Silk

In the last years of the twentieth century virtually the entire world contracted capitalism. Like an airborne virus, the spirit of free enterprise—of markets unhindered by government rule and regulation—blew across the face of the earth, not only settling in such unfamiliar precincts as Beijing and Moscow but also revisiting Great Britain and the United States, whence it originally arose. It was blown, first, by the collapse of the communist dream, and then by the collapse of the dream in action. At the end of 1991, the president of the Russian Republic, Boris Yeltsin, issued a declaration of Russia's independence from the Union of Soviet Socialist Republics, thereby pulling the rug out from under the largest experiment in economic history.

In 1992, my father embarked on a project for the Twentieth Century Fund to reckon with the future of capitalism. Now that the Cold War had come to an end, what would become of the economic system that had prevailed? How well would it deal with the new challenges, economic and political, that the world faced?

Of the perils he was well aware. When he was eleven, the Great Crash of 1929 wiped out his father, a clothing merchant addicted to buying stock on margin. The awareness that everything could be lost in a flash never left the son. But his experience as a teenager growing up during the New Deal left him, as well, with the confidence that strong political leadership and enlightened government intervention could make a difference. This confidence grew as his life progressed. In 1945, he reported on the founding of the United Nations for his divisional newspaper in Alaska. After World War II ended, he witnessed the reconstitution of the Northern European welfare state, writing his economics doctoral dissertation on Sweden's plans to provide better housing for its citizens. Working for the U.S. mission to NATO in the early 1950s, he was involved in supervising the economic reconstruction of Western Europe that had begun with the Marshall Plan.

For my father, the end of the Cold War at first seemed to hark back to those early, heady, postwar years. The enemies of freedom had been defeated; their economies lay prostrate. Here was a new opportunity for America to help fashion a better world, both through direct aid and by way of word and example.

It was not to be, at least not in his lifetime. The United States, hamstrung by huge budget deficits, was reluctant to spend its treasure abroad in the absence of any obvious threat to national security. Equally discouraging, the professional understanding of how to go about the business of economic reconstruction seemed to him to have all but disappeared since his salad days. His generation of economists, inspired by the theories of John Maynard Keynes and the practices of Franklin Delano Roosevelt, understood their highest task to be to devise government policies that would keep the world from ever again slipping into the kind of depression that had devastated it during the 1930s. The current generation, bemused by the elegancies of microeconomic theory, appeared to have lost interest in macroeconomic policy except insofar as it could be shown to be wrongheaded, ineffectual, or counterproductive. After World War II, American money and American expertise had helped set the Free World on a career of unprecedented growth and prosperity. Now that the entire world appeared to be moving into the Free World's camp, America seemed bankrupt, financially and intellectually.

The 1994 elections deepened his sense of American failure. Exhausted by the liver cancer to which he would succumb three months later, he spoke with disgust of the meanness of the Republicans' proposals, the glibness of their allegiance to a version of laissez faire well outside the mainstream of economics extending back to Adam Smith.

Professionally, he had devoted most of his working life to educating the public in economics and economic policy. At *Business Week* magazine, he was hired by Elliott V. Bell to inaugurate a department of economics. Bell, who had earlier held down the economic policy slot on the *New York Times* editorial board, was a Republican who wanted to teach the business community to look beyond its narrow self-interest, to understand that the Keynesian Revolution would make its world a better, more profitable place. This was the evangel that my father tried to spread at *Business Week,* where he eventually became editor of the editorial page. Later, as chief economics editorial writer and economics columnist at the *New York Times,* he was able to place it before a wider public. After the 1994 election, it almost seemed that he had labored in vain.

In the eyes of the new devotees of laissez faire, the very idea that the government should take responsibility for maintaining economic growth and assisting those the market economy leaves behind is a kind of socialist illusion. To them, it seems impossible to be at once enthusiastic about what markets can do and convinced of the need to remedy their defects. Instead, they have persuaded themselves that government intervention in the economy will always have bad unintended consequences—and that those consequences will necessarily outweigh any good that is accomplished.

Unlike a number of the free market's most devoted publicists today, my father never showed the slightest inclination toward socialism, from his student days at the University of Wisconsin in the late 1930s forward. But just as the eschatological vision of the workers' paradise left him cold, so too did the theology of the invisible hand, with its own paradisiac promises. Experience had taught him better—not just the experience of living through the Great Depression but the experience of economic journalism. There was no better vantage from which to take stock of the vast array of patent medicines that are always being purveyed for economic ills: the sure-fire investment advice, the cure-all best-sellers, the anodyne policy prescriptions, the latest academic panacea. It was not just because he could make economic policy comprehensible to noneconomists that his column was so widely valued across the political spectrum. Week in and week out, he let his readers in on a well-kept secret: Big economic problems rarely admit of simple solutions. As this, his last book, shows, that remains as true as ever in this era of capitalist triumph.

Several months after his death, I was asked by the Twentieth Century Fund's president, Richard Leone, if I would be willing to take charge of doing what had to be done to prepare my father's unfinished manuscript for publication. We agreed on the need to bring in additional authors to contribute chapters necessary to the argument. Besides the overall editing, what fell to me was to place the whole in the context of the Republican economic agenda that came into play in 1995. That agenda, which advanced simplistic free-market solutions to all the problems of post-Cold War economic life, became the touchstone, and intellectual foil, for examining the disparate forces pushing and pulling at the evolution of capitalism in today's world.

Jonas Pontusson of Cornell University and Bernard Wasow of the Ford Foundation not only worked hard and fast to complete their chapters, but also gave me the benefit of their expert insight and wise counsel. Robert Heilbroner was good enough to grace the book with his own distinctive perspective on the shape of capitalism in America. Tom Kono of the United Nations International University in Tokyo provided invaluable research assistance to my father early on, and important help to me at the end; the chapter on Japan could not have been done without him. Kathleen Quinn and Michael McGovern of the Twentieth Century Fund were there when I needed them. Above all, I would like to thank Richard Leone for enabling me to shepherd this project to completion, and for reassuring my father, in his last months, that one way or another his work would see the light of day.

I am also grateful to my former editors at the *Atlanta Journal-Constitution* for giving me the several months' leave I needed. It was a leave made doubly rewarding by the chance to spend more time than usual with my sons Abraham, Ezra, and Isaac, and with my wife Tema, at the end of a difficult year for all of us; I hope it helped them as much as it helped me. I had collaborated with my father on various earlier projects, but collaborating with him posthumously proved to be a moving and at times eerie experience; his prose was always before me, and I had only to close my eyes to hear his voice. As much as this was an act of filial piety, it was also, as usual when he was involved, filled with passion and fun. I trust he wouldn't mind that, for once, I had the last word.

Although he had his moments of doubt, Dad remained to the

end a creature of light—an optimist. He believed that people were basically good, and that they could be inspired to be better. The least dismal of dismal scientists, he saw economics as bearing not the grim news of scarcity but the hopeful promise of improving the lives of the poorest among us. He stood for the right as he saw the right. And if the rest of the world did not agree, well, in time it would come around.

ONE

··

The March of Capitalism

Leonard Silk and Mark Silk

hree years after the dream of communism guttered out in the ashes of the Soviet Union, the Republican Party won a majority of seats in both houses of the U.S. Congress and announced a new capitalist revolution. "[W]e have to replace the welfare state with an opportunity society," declared Newt Gingrich, the soon-to-be Speaker of the House of Representatives, just after the November 8, 1994, congressional elections. "It is impossible to take the Great Society structure of bureaucracy, the redistributionist model of how wealth is acquired, and the counterculture value system that now permeates the way we deal with the poor, and have any hope of fixing them. They are a disaster."[1]

Taking the helm of the first Republican-led House in more than forty years, Gingrich and company spent their first hundred days ramming through most of the Contract With America, the ten-bill legislative package that had served as their campaign platform. Texas congressman Dick Armey, the House Majority Leader and perhaps the truest believer, called it the Freedom Revolution, based on "the simple idea that people should be trusted to spend their own earnings and decide their own futures." The revolution would not entail any loss of fairness or kindness to the poor, for, according to Armey, "[t]he most just and compassionate societies, it turns out, are also the most free."[2] In order to liberate capitalist enterprise to work its wonders, the House Republicans proposed to roll back federal regulatory power and reduce federal outlays anywhere from one-third to one-half.

It could not happen right away. For two years, the revolutionaries in the House would have to contend with a Democratic president's veto power, as well as with less radical members of their own party who were unwilling to go along with the whole program. But after the next election, who knew? Would 1994 mark the beginning of a new era in American history, culminating in the election in 1996 of a president who would lead the country back to the days before Lyndon Johnson's Great Society, Franklin Delano Roosevelt's New Deal, or even Theodore Roosevelt's New Nationalism? Or would the revolution subside as an extraordinary but temporary midterm disturbance, brought about by a citizenry disgruntled with business as usual but unprepared to go along with a radical overhaul of the American system? At issue was the course of the country for years to come.

The House Republican agenda did not, of course, come forth in a vacuum. A retreat from the ideals of the New Deal had been underway at least since the presidency of Ronald Reagan. Nor was hostility to "big government" limited to the United States. In Great Britain during the 1980s, Prime Minister Margaret

Thatcher undertook to dismantle a welfare state far more extensive than anything ever attempted in the United States. Similarly if less aggressively, the advanced industrial states of Northern Europe were cutting back on the government economic supports and services of the postwar period. According to the prevailing wisdom, these could no longer be afforded if a country's businesses were to compete successfully in an increasingly international marketplace.

Thus, by the time the Soviet bloc began to break up in 1989, the loudest and most energetic economic voices were trumpeting a purer free-enterprise ideology than had been heard in many years, if ever. Small wonder that into the counsels of the leaders of the new ex-communist countries came free-market economists preaching a gospel of immediate deregulation, rapid privatization of state-owned enterprises, and the abandonment of employment guarantees.

The results were not as good as advertised. Economic prescriptions for "marketizing" the ex-communist countries tended to neglect the barriers to economic growth caused by the absence of the legal and regulatory structure of developed capitalist societies. Corruption, formerly endemic, became worse. Consummating business deals meant being subjected to demands for bribes and other forms of "lubrication." For masses of people, capitalism began to look like a bonanza for the few—especially the clever politicians, ex-bureaucrats, and the new mafia. A common joke in Russia was that capitalism overnight had succeeded in doing what the Kremlin in seventy years had failed to do: make communism look good.

Falling output and income together with growing unemployment and poverty raised the specter that aggressive nationalism, ethnic hostility, and political instability would lead to repressive dictatorships and new dangers of war, civil and international. In the transition from communism, there was widespread tension and anxiety about the future among those who had thus far suffered from the collapse of the old order. Bitterness and even nostalgia for the communist past grew among people raised on an ideology of equality and job security guaranteed by the state. Victories by former Communists and reconstituted communist parties in much of the former Soviet bloc in the mid-1990s were a measure of popular disaffection with the new economic order.

To be sure, despite the economic failures and the devastating effects on their well-being, there seemed little desire on the part of the majority to go back to even one of the more benign variants of Cold War communism, much less to full-blown Stalinist totalitarianism. Few wished a return of the cruelty and arrogance, the spying and harassment, the repressed inflation and the long waiting lines, the poor quality of goods and services and housing, the meanness and hopelessness of life for so many. But on the basis of their experiences since the fall of communism, citizens of the former communist world wanted to know whether that system called capitalism was too selfish, corrupt, and cold-blooded to meet their needs. Still looking for a democratic-market system that works, they asked: What sort of system should that be?

Models of Capitalism

While many economies marked by private ownership of capital and by open trading in free markets exist, a closer look reveals that there is not one capitalist model but many "capitalisms." In every capitalist nation, the economic system has been shaped by particular historical, social, and cultural forces and by politically determined national needs. There is thus a long menu of models to choose from:

- *The libertarian or laissez-faire model* restricts the role of the state largely to defense, with minimal or no intervention in economic and social matters.

- *The neoclassical model* lets the market resolve most microeconomic issues within a general regulatory regime, while employing national fiscal and monetary policy to varying degrees to achieve macroeconomic stability, low inflation and/or high employment.

- *The mixed economy, welfare state, or social market economy* blends government and private market decisions to resolve clashes between economic interests and social needs, particularly to insure a "social safety net" for those who fail in the market economy.

- In *the corporate state,* business and government work closely together, whether overtly or covertly, honestly or corruptly, to pursue national and business interests.

- Finally, in *authoritarian and totalitarian systems,* a powerful government preserves the market and promotes the interests of favored businesses, but represses genuine democracy and personal freedom.

Within these broad categories, there are various subspecies of capitalism, varying not only from country to country but, within a country, from time to time. For example, Middle Eastern states like Syria, Iran, and Iraq have in recent years taken a fascist approach, with the state dominating private enterprise. In such states, an asserted need to prevent internal instability and to repel outside aggressors is used to justify one degree or another of political dictatorship, while the desire to trade with other countries and gain the benefits of technological advance necessitates experimenting with capitalist institutions.

China's success, at least until now, in achieving economic growth rates of double-digit proportions by combining strong state political control with an expanding capitalist sector may provide a model that some countries will be tempted to imitate. Indeed, many ex-communist societies are asking themselves: Isn't oppressive government with economic liberalization in the Chinese style more desirable than chaotic democratization *à la Russe,* at least during what is likely to be a long transition period?

The effort of the ex-communist countries to figure out their capitalist futures is not made easier by the fact that the longtime capitalist countries are also in the midst of a struggle to find better ways of combining market forces with assurances of human security. While many northern European countries continue to trim their welfare states, Great Britain is acting to reverse the Thatcherite free-market revolution. In Japan, the power of the government to orchestrate economic activity and keep the masses subservient has come increasingly into question, though the results of that questioning remain to be seen. And if the United States turns back the clock as far as the House Republicans proposed in 1995, the result would be a degree of laissez faire unknown for generations anywhere in the industrialized world.

How far should the state go to insulate its citizens from volatile market forces? If the state is to be the agency for guiding social and economic development, how can it be stopped from degenerating into corrupt cliques of politicians and bureaucrats? Around the globe, finding the right systemic answers involves the quest not only for economic efficiency but also for other goals that may serve the public interest.

What is the public interest? Is it simply the sum of all private interests? Or, considering the clashes among individuals and groups and the wide disparities among them in income and wealth and power, should it be defined in terms of some larger principles, such as equality, social stability, humanitarian purpose, or economic progress itself?

Perhaps the resolution of clashing interests and values is best left to the market, not because its solutions are necessarily just or compassionate but because market outcomes (whether rewards or punishments) usually produce better results for the entire society than the decisions of politicians and the interests they represent (including their own interests as people in power). Doesn't politics, whatever its intentions or pretensions, inevitably serve the interests of the most powerful elements or class in the society? Yet even if free markets in general work tolerably well, and certainly better than highly centralized political command-and-control systems, shouldn't nations take steps to supplement and correct their malfunctioning to meet the needs of all citizens—especially those who are poorest and in greatest need of help?

Whatever the case, the economics of a system cannot be divorced from moral issues, including the obligations of the rich to the poor, the responsibility of the current generation to those yet unborn, and the proper extent and limits of individual rights and freedoms. Addressing the interplay of economics and such issues at the current moment of worldwide capitalist triumph is the purpose of this book.

The Capitalist Ethic

Does capitalism have an ethic, joined to human freedom, that addresses social concerns and needs as the indirect consequence of individuals' pursuit of their own economic interests? Or, in its narrow focus on self-interest, is capitalism the nemesis of ethics?

Capitalism was originally assaulted, almost a thousand years ago, on moral grounds. Centuries before it acquired a name or a theory, medieval theologians sensed its revolutionary nature and the danger it posed to the social, religious, and moral order. As early as the twelfth century, the stiffening attitude of the Roman Catholic church toward usury represented an awareness of the threat of this new and powerful force to the medieval ideal of a harmoniously ordered society.

It was usury—the payment of interest, making it possible to earn money on money—that brought capital into being and launched capitalism upon its revolutionary career. No wonder the guardians of the medieval order of values were against it, said the Catholic historian Werner Stark:

> [For here] was the cancerous cell which, if not excised from the body politic by the surgeon's knife, would grow ever more rap-idly until it had eaten out the vitals and brought on destruction and death. It has been said more than once that the Doctors did not understand the phenomenon of capital, but that is decidedly less than fair. Certainly, they did not have an express theory of it, but they realized, however dimly, what its true nature is—to be the spring of economic change and advancement, to be the motor force of progress. Here again the contrast between medieval and modern conceptions becomes strikingly obvious. We think eco-nomic progress desirable, whatever the cost; they counted the cost and found it excessive.[3]

Adam Smith, the eighteenth-century Scottish philosopher whose *Wealth of Nations* inaugurated modern economics, saw capitalism as grounded not in an immoral thirst for gain but in the basic human propensity to "truck, barter, and exchange one thing for another." This propensity enabled people to depend upon one another for their needs without having to beg. "It is not from the benevolence of the butcher, the brewer, or the baker, that we expect our dinner, but from their regard to their own interest," Smith wrote. "We address ourselves, not to their humanity but to their self-love, and never talk to them of our own necessities but of their advantages."[4] Neither moral nor immoral, the habit of exchange brought about the division of labor that, on Smith's account, was the chief producer of wealth.

Later, capitalism rose well above ethical neutrality, at least in the eyes of some. At the dawn of the twentieth century, the German sociologist Max Weber portrayed it as the secular expression of a social theology; he pointed to the Calvinist concept of a person's "calling," which was not the role in which he had been placed by Heaven but the earthly business he chose for himself and would pursue with religious fervor. The obligation to work hard, to be thrifty and responsible, to save and invest money prudently, never to deplete one's capital but always to enlarge it, acquired sanctity as "the Protestant ethic."[5]

Whether immoral, amoral, or the height of virtue, the capitalist creed has been most succinctly and pragmatically enunciated in our own time by the Chinese Communist leader Deng Xiaoping, who told his people: "To get rich is glorious." What capitalism represented was a radical change in the power relations within society—in the first instance, from the ruling class of feudal lords, whose power was supported by the church, to merchants and bankers who knew how to accumulate capital not just by making things but by making money beget money. The members of this new dominant class put their capital to work primarily for their own enrichment but with side benefits to the state, which often won them the support of the prince. With the passage of time, the wealth generated by capital spread through society, such that it was ultimately possible to persuade workers themselves to identify their own interests with those of the capitalists. An American propaganda campaign early in the Cold War sought to rename the system "people's capitalism."

Despite its protean ability to adapt itself to enormously different political systems, capitalism does have certain characteristics that make it recognizable wherever it appears:

- the existence of private property—the ownership (or at least control) of assets by entities other than the state, and the ability of those private owners to capture the returns on their investment of capital;
- freedom of enterprise—the right of individual capitalists to start new businesses or change, expand, or get out of their existing businesses;
- the profit motive—or more broadly, the desire for economic gain—as the dominant force behind individual and business behavior; and
- decentralized decisionmaking by way of free competition in the marketplace as the spur to efficiency and the creation of new and more attractive goods and services.

Of course, only in the textbook model of perfect competition and "pure" capitalism do all of these characteristics exist without some interference or control of the state or of monopolies and cartels in the private sector, frequently with government support or protection.

Capitalism is above all intensely "rational," with its rationality commonly defined as the pursuit of pecuniary self-interest—and with more always preferable to less. Some economists go so far as to define the pursuit of gain as the only form of rational behavior. In any event, one can hardly overestimate the power of this form of rationality to transform the world—not only economic life but science and culture and religion as well. As the conservative Viennese economist Joseph Schumpeter wrote:

> Primarily a product of the evolution of economic rationality, the cost-price calculus in turn reacts upon that rationality; by crystallizing and defining numerically, it powerfully propels the logic of enterprise. And thus defined and quantified for the economic sector, this type of logic or attitude or method then starts upon its conquering career subjugating—rationalizing—man's tools and philosophies, his medical practice, his picture of the cosmos, his outlook on life, everything in fact including the concepts of beauty and justice and his spiritual ambitions.[6]

Small wonder that capitalism, wherever it has taken root, has failed to win universal approval as the best or only road to a good society.

Why Capitalism Won

No one appreciated the power of capitalism to transform the world better than its foremost enemy, Karl Marx. In *The Communist Manifesto*, Marx (and his colleague Friedrich Engels) wrote:

> The bourgeoisie, by the rapid improvement of all instruments of production, by the immensely facilitated means of communication, draws all, even the most barbarian, nations into civilization. The cheap prices of its commodities are the heavy artillery with which it batters down all Chinese walls, with which it forces the barbarians' intensely obstinate hatred of foreigners to capitulate. It compels all nations, on pain of extinction, to adopt the bourgeois mode of production; it compels them to introduce what it calls civilization into their midst, i.e., to become bourgeois themselves. In one word, it creates a world after its own image.[7]

Marx and Engels saw capitalism not as a benign God who promoted the interests of humankind with an invisible hand but as a tyrannical demiurge wielding an iron fist on behalf of the controllers of capital—the bourgeoisie. In capitalist countries, governments were a tool of the bourgeoisie, designed to hold down the working class with the support of the police and the military. To stop bourgeois civilization in its tracks a communist revolution was required. It would be aided by the inherent instability of capitalism: by depressions that caused the system to break down, and by the progressive immiseration of the exploited working class.

But the communist revolution failed because the capitalist system proved capable of bringing not immiseration but progressively higher living standards to the workers; because economists, led by John Maynard Keynes, devised means for damping down and containing the wild swings of the business cycle; and because the centrally controlled economies established by communist regimes could not keep pace with capitalist countries committed to invention and innovation, with the United States in the forefront.

In its relatively short history, America has had four great waves of growth, each lasting a little more than half a century. The first, based on iron, steam power, and cotton textiles, lasted from the end of the American Revolution until the 1840s. The second, based on railroads and steel, lasted until the end of the 1890s. The third, driven by electricity, the automobile, and oil, lasted until about the middle of the twentieth century. The fourth wave, which has not yet been exhausted—and which could roll on indefinitely—got under way during the Second World War. It was based not on a few technological innovations but on a host of discoveries stemming from scientific progress in electronics and computers, the biological sciences, nuclear and solid-state physics, organic and inorganic chemistry, engineering, aeronautics, astrophysics, the earth sciences, and mathematics.

What we are passing through might be called the Research Revolution, a sophisticated and profound outgrowth of the Industrial Revolution. Doubtless the most important factor in launching this new revolution, in which basic science emerged as the initiator of industrial, social, and political change, was the success of organized research on military problems in World War II. Early in the war British scientists moved into high positions in their government and industry to attack a wide variety of problems. Shortly thereafter in the United States, the Office of Scientific Research and Development performed the same function and initiated many of the wonders crucial to Allied victory. The war brought into being radar, antibiotics, and the first electronic computers. But the most dramatic and militarily significant development was, of course, the Manhattan Project, which enlisted the knowledge and talents of many refugee and American-born scientists to create the atomic bomb before our enemies got it.

The end of World War II quickly ushered in the great ideological confrontation of the victors. The communists, led by the Soviet Union, resumed their intention of making a world revolution; the non-communist powers, led by the United States, declared their intention to prevent it. Never before had the entire world been thus divided between two colossal powers locked in apparently permanent conflict. With thermonuclear weapons in the possession of both sides, direct, full-scale military conflict between them became unthinkable. Hence the Cold War, a contest no less bitter for being fought in surrogate countries along the long periphery between the capitalist and communist empires and, at a distance, by spying, feinting, occasional terror, propaganda—and economics.

The old Marxist-Leninist thesis held that a capitalist country like the United States, facing falling rates of return on capital at home, needed war to exploit new opportunities for profit abroad and to create prosperity and high employment at home. The truth is that the Cold War supplied a military rationale for the United States to keep the Research Revolution going, through massive government funding of basic research in universities and private corporate research and development. When the Soviet Union launched its first space satellite, Sputnik, in 1957, the United States responded not only with its own space program but also by infusing the nation's education system with money for training a generation of scientists and engineers. If the most glorious expression of this effort was the Apollo moon mission, its last hurrah was the Strategic Defense Initiative (SDI), popularly known as Star Wars. SDI, which sought to place America beyond the reach of the Soviet Union's balance of terror, was the capstone of the post-Vietnam military build-up that began under President Carter and greatly accelerated under President Reagan.

Reagan-era hawks credited this build-up with breaking the back of the Soviet Union and ending the Cold War, but that view may be doubted.[8] In his recent memoirs, the former Soviet ambassador to the United States, Anatoly Dobrynin, argues plausibly that a hard-line Soviet regime could easily have maintained its side of the arms race and kept the Cold War going: "Sadly for the ardent followers of Reagan, the increased Soviet defense spending provoked by Reagan's policies was not the straw that broke the back of the evil empire. We did not bankrupt ourselves in the arms race, as the Caspar Weinbergers of this world would like to believe. The Soviet response to Star Wars caused only an acceptable small rise in defense spending." What is undeniable, however, is that Western capitalism had been able to afford an extensive military establishment and an expensive arms race while still increasing the well-being of its citizens; Soviet-style communism had not. As Dobrynin notes, "The troubles in our economy were the result of our own internal contradictions of autarky, low investment, and lack of innovation. . . . "[9] What the long Cold War did was provide plenty of time for the West to forge ahead economically, and the East to sink.

In the Soviet Union, the economy was collapsing in on itself. It has been estimated that in 1975, only 15 percent of investment in the Russian Republic was going to consumer industries. Political and economic corruption was growing apace as party bosses, secure under the aging Leonid Brezhnev, made lining their own pockets their foremost goal. Meanwhile, the entire system had become dependent on a "shadow" economy of unofficial buy and barter that accounted for as much as one-third of all economic activity.[10] Nor was it simply in the arena of basic goods that the Communist system was failing. Culturally, rock 'n' roll, blue jeans, and other icons of capitalist decadence were battering down the Iron Curtain and winning the hearts of Soviet youth.

In the face of these woes, there was growing internal awareness that the only remedy was a healthy dose of market incentives. Indeed, even before he became general secretary of the Communist Party in 1985, Mikhail Gorbachev spoke publicly of the need for decentralization of economic power—perestroika.[11] Not that Gorbachev had any intention of doing away with communism, much less with the Soviet Union. He was a reformer who believed that greater freedom of expression and a more democratic approach to decisionmaking would promote the economic progress that was necessary. "More socialism, more democracy," was how he liked to put it. His goal was a social market economy akin to Sweden's, combining elements of capitalism and socialism.[12]

After his initial efforts to restructure the economy with cooperatives and "individual work activities" proved fruitless, Gorbachev moved toward more thoroughgoing reforms. At the June, 1987, plenum of the Central Committee, he announced his intention to make every enterprise self-supporting, to introduce a new, rational price structure, and to create a new system of finance and credit so that enterprises could borrow money for investment. This economic order would be in place by 1991, his chief economic adviser said. To many in the West, that seemed too fast. Margaret Thatcher herself told Gorbachev during a visit to Moscow in the spring of 1987 that high officials in the Reagan administration were concerned that perestroika would excessively disrupt the workings of the huge Soviet economy. Based on her own difficulties privatizing industry in Great Britain, she wished the Soviet leader well but warned him to go slow.[13]

Many Western experts recognized the immense complexity of the task Gorbachev had set for himself. There would have to be financial stabilization; a decontrol of prices and quantities; selective demonopolization; a transfer of assets from state ownership to other proprietors; and an opening up of the economy to competition from imported products and foreign investment. Arranging all this in a nondisruptive sequence would be exceedingly difficult. Meanwhile, it would take time to create the institutions and skills of a market economy.[14]

But inside Russia, patience for gradualism was rapidly wearing thin. Far from strengthening socialism, Gorbachev's program of free speech and democratization had succeeded only in opening the floodgates of criticism, in weakening central authority to bring about reform, and in animating the desire for independence among nations that in some cases had been part of the Russian empire for hundreds of years. Effectively, Gorbachev was destroying the system he had hoped to reform.

In 1990, he turned for yet another economic reform plan to Stanislav Shatalin, an aging economist who had repeatedly run afoul of previous regimes for advocating radical reform. "[I]s this just another case of 'improving socialism' or creating a 'controlled market'?" Shatalin asked. "Because if it is, I'm a sick man and I don't have time left for such follies. But if you are serious now, I'm ready."[15] The Shatalin plan, which Gorbachev first endorsed, then rejected, proposed to privatize no less than 80 percent of the Soviet Union's economic enterprises within 500 days. In the final year of the Gorbachev regime, the economy went from bad to worse, as hyperinflation and chronic shortages overtook a command economy in which fewer and fewer enterprises were obeying the commands.

Even among the stalwarts of the old regime, there was recognition that a market economy had to be embraced. In July, 1991, just before the abortive military coup that sent the Soviet Union into its final tailspin, the Politburo, following Gorbachev's lead for the last time, endorsed private property, private farming, and retail trade. It was not economic liberalization that provoked the coup, but rather the treaty that would have transformed the Soviet Union into a federation of independent republics. But just as Gorbachev's effort to maintain a political role for central authority within such a federation had become an unacceptable halfway house, so his economic vision of a middle path between central planning and laissez faire had lost whatever appeal it might once have had to the younger generation of reformers.

Before the denouement, a visitor called on Anatoly Chubais, Leningrad's deputy mayor for economic policy. Noticing a bare spot on the wall where there should have been a portrait of the current Soviet leader, the visitor asked whose portrait he intended to hang there. "Mm . . . . " Chubais replied. "Let me think about it. No doubt some economist. Well, let's say Friedman or Hayek."[16]

Those two, Milton Friedman and Friedrich von Hayek, were the patriarchs of the laissez-faire counter-revolution in the West. For his part, Chubais would soon be First Deputy Premier and chief economic strategist of the new post-communist Russia.

TWO

···

The Challenge of
Slow Growth

Leonard Silk and Mark Silk

I n a sense, the Cold War could not have come to an end at a worse time. At the very moment of capitalism's triumph, the industrialized Free World was entering a painful and protracted economic slowdown such as had not been experienced since the end of World War II. This international recession exacerbated impulses to nationalism, regionalism, and protectionism, and increased the strains upon social cohesion around the world.

The growth rate of the industrial countries fell from 4.4 percent in 1988 to 3.3 percent in 1989, 2.6 percent in 1990, 0.9 percent in 1991, and 1.7 percent in 1992—too slow to keep pace with the growth of the labor force. Unemployment rose above 10 percent in most of Europe and in Canada, and above 7 percent in the United States.[1]

Meanwhile, the combined growth rate of the "economies in transition"—the former Soviet Union and Eastern Europe—fell from 4.5 percent in 1988 to 2.3 percent in 1989. It then went negative, plummeting by 5 percent in 1990, 15.9 percent in 1991, and 12 percent in 1992—a decline of one-third of total output in three years that represented a steeper fall than any country or combination of countries suffered in the Great Depression of the 1930s. Systemic collapse in the East aggravated problems in the West—especially the huge influx of immigrants to Western Europe.

But the slowdown in the West did not begin with the collapse of the Soviet empire, the end of the financial boom of the 1980s, or the 1987 stock market crash. Rather, it started two decades earlier with the beginning of a persistent decline in productivity, whether measured by output per worker hour or by all factors of production.

The slowdown in productivity growth is evident in the data for all of the "Big Seven" members of the Organization for Economic Cooperation and Development (OECD): the United States, Japan, Germany, the United Kingdom, Italy, France, and Canada. The annual growth of U.S. gross domestic product, per capita, dropped from an average of two percent in 1955–73 to 1.3 percent in 1973–86. In the same two periods, Japan's per capita GDP fell from 8.8 percent to 3.3 percent, Germany's from 4.2 percent to 2 percent, and the combined rate of the other four members of the Big Seven from 3.8 percent to 1.7 percent. One may argue about the precise measurements but not about the overall downslide of productivity growth that has been going on for two decades.

Lingering Impact of Oil Shocks

What caused the productivity slowdown? Economists are still not sure. Their principal explanation, especially because of the timing, is the oil-price explosions of 1973 and 1979. Other leading suspects are an asserted greater rigidity of national economic systems, a fall-off in the growth of new knowledge and technology, and tax systems (particularly in the United States) that favor consumption, discriminate against saving, and retard investment.[2]

Low savings and investment rates clearly weakened America's productivity growth and overall economic performance. In the 1980s, America's net national savings rate fell from about 8 percent of national income in the preceding three decades to less than 3 percent because of large federal deficits and lower private savings. That meant that proportionally the United States was saving far less than any other major industrial country: about one-fifth Japan's net savings rate and one-third that of Germany and the Group of Seven as a whole. The shortage of savings not only constrained American growth but also severely limited the capital the United States could supply to developing countries or to the ex-communist states struggling to build market economies and effective democracies.

The economic causes of the inflation and the productivity slowdown simply cannot be separated from political ones. The oil shocks were tied to growing Western dependence on Middle Eastern oil; they were triggered by Arab states using oil as a weapon against Western importers following the 1973 Arab-Israeli war, and then by the Ayatollah Khomeini's Iranian revolution in 1979. These price explosions were also linked to economic boom and worldwide commodity-price inflation kicked off by the escalation of the Vietnam War, and to the failure of the Johnson administration to take prompt fiscal action, either by domestic spending cuts or tax increases, to head off inflation. This dilatory fiscal action resulted from President Johnson's unwillingness either to curb domestic spending by gutting Great

Society programs or to demand a tax increase to finance the Vietnam War—as well as from his desire to push for economic growth.

The U.S. inflation, born in Vietnam, became global. Excess fiscal and monetary stimulus on the part of other developed countries also contributed to the worldwide commodity boom of the late sixties and early seventies. Inflation in the industrial countries worsened the terms of trade of Third World and Middle Eastern oil producers, setting the stage for the first round of oil-price hikes. Rising oil prices fueled general inflation and forced the developed countries to adopt the tight monetary and fiscal policies that would in turn intensify the investment, productivity and output slowdowns of the 1970s, 1980s, and 1990s.

In the 1980s, the effect of the oil shocks on productivity growth gradually wore off; industrial nations, some faster than others, adjusted to higher oil prices; and the *relative* world oil price came down. Nevertheless, the slow rate of productivity growth continued. Hence, the causes of slow growth in the late 1980s and early 1990s had to lie elsewhere.

Deflating "Bubbles" Slowed Growth

Speculative fever gripped stock markets and real estate markets in the 1980s and caused a global wave of mergers and acquisitions. Rapid growth of the world's financial markets and an increasingly anti-government political climate that reduced financial and antitrust supervision and regulation combined to produce "bubbles" in economies around the world. Lest the bubbles burst, governments and central banks decided to let some air out of them. But deflationary actions—not only by financial regulators but also by private financial institutions themselves—aggravated the economic slowdown.

In Germany, the fall of the Berlin Wall exacerbated the switch to counterinflationary measures. The huge price of the "takeover bid" paid by Chancellor Helmut Kohl to bring about quick unification—an exchange of West German marks for East German marks at an overpriced one-to-one rate and a transfer of capital to the East amounting to about $100 billion a year—caused the German budget to swing from a moderate surplus in 1989 to a deficit equal to 5 percent of gross domestic product in 1992. That set off inflationary pressures and, even worse, inflationary fears.

To still the pressures and fears, the Bundesbank—true to the inflation-phobia that has afflicted Germany ever since the hyperinflation of the early 1920s—kept money tight and interest rates high while the rest of Europe was trying to fight recession. European currencies yoked to the German mark became increasingly overvalued. The result was to worsen the problem of slow growth in Europe and everywhere else. Bundesbank policy also intensified disequilibrium among currencies and political strains among European Community signatories of the 1992 Maastricht Treaty, threatening European monetary and political integration and even the world trading system under the General Agreement on Tariffs and Trade (GATT).

On the other side of the world, Japan was experiencing the worst economic and political tensions and anxieties since beginning its remarkable postwar recovery and its long spell of rapid growth. Its financial bubble, built on booming asset values, was sharply deflated; stock and real estate prices fell precipitously. Scandals over political and business corruption shook public confidence in the system as the economic slump intensified public discontent and even anger with the country's political leader-

ship. The Japanese establishment—including politicians, bureaucrats, and business leaders—acknowledged that the country
was in a genuine recession and warned that the strains might
last five to seven years longer, and possibly a decade or more.

The fear was that the steep fall of securities prices, real estate,
and other asset values would have a long-lasting effect on Japanese banks and industries. In 1992, one senior Japanese economist said: "In the past the threats were like a broken leg—sharp,
painful but specific—and it was clear what was needed to mend
them. This downturn is more like a virus affecting the blood
system—much more complex and pervasive."[3] The same year,
Akio Mikuni, a leading Japanese financial analyst, noted that in
its efforts to cure the disease Japan's powerful Ministry of Finance was caught in a dilemma: "If it allows the prices of land
and equity to be set genuinely by market forces, asset prices
would plummet and the capital cushion of Japan's banks wiped
out. The Finance Ministry would have given up its most important tools right at the moment they would be needed for
coping with a resultant first-order banking crisis. If, however,
assets continue to be supported at unrealistically high levels, the
underlying deterioration of both the financial sector and the
profitability of manufacturing industries will only worsen." Mikuni considered unsustainable the Finance Ministry's decision to
support the markets at their deteriorated levels: "The negative
carrying costs of holding overpriced assets will continue to eat
away not just at the stability of the financial sector but also at the
profitability of manufacturing firms."[4]

Other analysts, while conceding that Japan had "finally gone
over the edge," believed that within a few years it would come
back stronger than ever. Kenneth S. Courtis, strategist and senior
economist for the Deutsche Bank Group in Asia, contended in

1992 that Japan was "purging itself of the excesses of the 1980s, cleansing its economy, melting off the fat" accumulated over recent years. "By the mid-1990s," Courtis said, "once the economy is brought down again to its rock-hard, competitive core, Japan will be poised for another powerful leap ahead through to the end of the decade."[5]

By late 1995, Mikuni looked to be the better prophet. In September, the Japanese government announced a package of $140 billion in spending and loan programs to get the economy going again. Analysts nonetheless remained dubious that even this, the largest of seven stimulative efforts since 1992, would be sufficient to do the trick. Meanwhile, real estate prices had shrunk to less than 50 percent of their bubble highs, leaving Japanese banks staggering under a burden of bad loans estimated at anywhere between $500 million and $1 trillion. In October, after a succession of bank failures, the U.S. Federal Reserve System agreed to provide the Japanese with dollars backed by U.S. Treasury bills lest the failures spark an international financial crisis. However long it took Japan to get back on track, it seemed clear that its recovery would depend not just on actions by the Ministry of Finance, the Ministry of International Trade and Industry, and other Japanese agencies, banks, and businesses but on the policies of foreign governments and developments in the world economy as a whole.

Like a Depression

Economists, financial analysts, government officials, and central bankers agreed that what was going on was not a typical business-cycle recession, either in Japan, Europe, or the United States. After a meeting with Japanese Prime Minister Kiichi Miyazawa and officials from the Ministry of Finance and Bank of Japan in October, 1992, Federal Reserve Board Chairman Alan Greenspan noted that among the topics discussed was "the balance sheet problem"—the problem of excessive indebtedness that in Japan is referred to as "asset deflation."[6] Greenspan had earlier described the structural imbalances in the U.S. economy as more severe and enduring than many had previously thought. The economy, he said, was "still recuperating from past excesses involving a generalized overreliance on debt to finance asset accumulation. Many of these activities were based largely on inflated expectations of future asset prices and income growth."[7]

As reality broke through, businesses and individuals holding debt-burdened balance sheets diverted cash flows to debt repayment at the expense of spending, while lenders turned cautious. The credit crunch was on, and, as Greenspan put it, "This phenomenon is not unique to the United States; similar adjustments have spread to Japan, Canada, Australia, the United Kingdom, and a number of northern European countries. For the first time in a half century or more, several industrial countries have been confronted at roughly the same time with asset-price deflation and the inevitable consequences."

The last such asset deflation, credit crunch, and wave of bankruptcies followed the Great Crash of 1929. Fiscal, monetary, and trade-policy blunders helped to turn that earlier bust into the worldwide Great Depression of the 1930s, which lasted a full decade—until the outbreak of World War II. In the phrase of the late editor of *Business Week*, Elliott V. Bell, "Out of the wreckage of depression slithered the serpents of Nazism and war." Nowadays, inverting the celebrated maxim of George Santayana, we believe, or hope, that those of us who do remember the past will not be condemned to repeat it.

The burst of optimism that greeted the downfall of Soviet communism quickly gave way to anxiety that years would pass before the new states of the East could become effective market economies and democracies—and that some might not make it at all before dictatorship returned. The end of the Cold War was expected to bring great benefits to people in many countries as resources were shifted from military to social programs. Instead, the peace dividend was being paid out in lost jobs and falling incomes.

Theoretically there was no reason why this had to be so. In a rational world, the improved prospects for peace should have led to greater spending on consumer goods and productivity-raising investment. But that happens only when workers can be shifted to new jobs—and financial resources reallocated to create those jobs. In the absence of sufficient shifts of human and capital resources to expanding civilian industries, there were strong economic pressures on arms-producing nations to maintain high levels of military production and to sell weapons—conventional as well as dual-use nuclear technology—wherever buyers could be found. Without a revival of national economies and of the global economy, the production and proliferation of weapons would continue, creating more Iraqs, Cambodias, Yugoslavias, and Somalias—or worse.

Like the Great Depression, the economic slump of the early 1990s fanned the fires of nationalist, ethnic, and religious hatred around the world. Economic hardship was not the only cause of these social and political pathologies, but it aggravated all of them, and in turn they fed back upon economic development. They also undermined efforts to deal with such global problems as environmental pollution, the production and trafficking of drugs, crime, sickness, famine, AIDS, and other plagues.

Economic growth would not solve all those problems. But growth—and growth alone—creates the additional resources that make it possible to achieve such fundamental goals as higher living standards, national and collective security, a healthier environment, and more open economies and societies.

Promoting Growth

What would it take to fuel the engines of economic growth in the post-Cold War era? The answer was the same lesson learned during the Great Depression: The developed capitalist countries needed to pursue macroeconomic policies that would keep the world economy moving forward and keep world trade and investment flowing freely. Specifically, five steps were needed:

- First, the United States and most other industrial countries had to increase savings and productive investment. A higher rate of capital formation in the industrial countries would serve not only their own interests but also, through the global growth mechanism of expanded markets, those of the developing countries, the newly industrialized countries of Asia, and the new states of Eastern Europe and the former Soviet Union. Higher rates of capital formation in the developing and newly market-oriented economies were critical not only to their economic success but to their political viability.
- Second, to play a constructive role in capital formation, the United States, still the largest and most important economy in the world, had to eliminate its huge budget deficits, which had forced it to import capital from abroad to finance government activities and help cover its own investment

needs. Instead of exporting capital to the developing world, with reciprocal benefits to its own exporting industries, the United States was absorbing capital from abroad, putting upward pressure on long-term interest rates and slowing its own and worldwide investment and growth.

- Third, U.S. economic policy also needed to raise the rate of national saving at least to its pre-1980 level of about 8 percent of national income, about five percentage points above its current level. The additional saving, when productively invested in new plant and equipment, research and development, and infrastructure, both public and private, would raise the annual growth rate of productivity back to its historic level of more than 2 percent per year; that would make possible a steady increase in living standards and extra capital for meeting domestic and foreign needs.

- Fourth, in a more closely integrated and stagnating world economy, the inadequate growth of the world money supply—not just of any single nation's money supply—needed to be addressed. Collaboration among the three most important central banks and sources of international monetary reserves—the Federal Reserve, the Bundesbank, and the Bank of Japan—would be vital to curbing world inflation or deflation and achieving stronger and steadier world economic growth. But collaboration by nations and their central banks on monetary policy had to be accompanied by efforts of national administrations and legislatures to coordinate fiscal policy, from which monetary policy could not be divorced.

- Finally, international cooperation had to be sought for reducing military spending to levels appropriate to the post-

Cold War environment. If defense budgets continued to be treated as employment-security or growth-stimulus programs, with spending levels rationalized by misapplied economic arguments, it would not only waste resources needed for investment and growth but also create pressures for otherwise unnecessary tax increases—and heighten threats to world peace and economic development.

The long-term problem made acute by globalization—and global slow growth, stagnating real output and income, overcapacity, and unemployment—was not just maintaining an adequate demand for goods and services but raising investment in activities that generated strong productivity growth and jobs. Increasing savings, per se, would not automatically raise the level of domestic investment sufficiently, although greater savings would help to reduce interest rates and thereby encourage investment. In the integrated global economy, capital saved in one country could as readily be invested abroad as at home; and, increasingly, business organizations and nations had to create or acquire the capital, human skills, and technological knowledge they would need to meet international competition. The alternative, protectionism and an aggressive nationalism, would endanger both peace and prosperity.

In fact, the interdependence resulting from economic integration greatly reduced the effective autonomy of even large national economies. Nations found that their policies were less potent domestically, affected other countries more strongly, and produced sharp and often unwelcome changes in the trade and payments balances and exchange rates that linked them with others. All this made cooperation among the major economies in policy-making increasingly important. Indeed, it could be argued that the greatest change needed to preserve stability and nurture growth was for the world economy to become the focus of policy formulation.

After World War II, every Western capitalist country accepted, formally or de facto, the responsibility of employing macroeconomic policies to combat inflation and unemployment—although, under varying economic and political pressures, nations weighted the two objectives differently. Throughout most of the postwar period, the need to contain and defeat Soviet communism went far to overcome political opportunism, the pressures of interest groups, and the inherent unpredictability of capitalist economic systems. As a result, the earlier postwar performance of the industrial nations was much better than in the years between World Wars I and II, when their beggar-thy-neighbor economic policies dragged the world into depression.

But with the dawn of the post-Cold War era, slow growth in the world economy made the danger of a reversion to beggar-thy-neighbor policies a real one. Some saw the three major economic powers, the United States, Germany, and Japan, riding in different directions, and threatening to pull the world economy apart.[8] Around the world, resistance to the principles of free trade was on the rise, and in the developed countries, there was increasing pressure to heighten barriers to immigration. Not entirely consistently, the new enthusiasm for laissez-faire ideology in the West made governments less ready to make use of the instruments of macroeconomic policy domestically—much less on a cooperative international basis.

The irony of the post-Cold War era was thus that the removal of Soviet communism from the world scene deprived the West of the strongest spur to economic cooperation at a time when such cooperation was needed more urgently than ever. And all countries—developed and developing, ex-communist and still formally Communist—were left to grope for forms of capitalism that would enable them to survive and prosper in the world economy without destroying the cultural values and power relationships that governed their ways of life.

THREE

···

American Contracts

Leonard Silk and Mark Silk

I n many countries, East and West, developed and developing, the terms "capitalist" and "capitalism" remain pejorative, synonymous with greed and selfishness. But in others, especially the United States, the terms are honorific. Many Americans identify capitalism with Americanism and consider competing economic "isms," whether socialism, communism, or feudalism, as by definition anti-American.

In fact, much of the world sees the United States as the epitome of capitalism, and rightly so. For here, the passion for growth, founded on technological progress and free enterprise, became virtually a national religion. In *The Protestant Ethic and the Spirit of Capitalism*, Max Weber was contemptuous of what he regarded as the abandonment by America of what he considered capitalism's "highest spiritual and cultural values." He wrote:

33

In the field of its highest development, in the United States, the pursuit of wealth, stripped of its religious and ethical meaning, tends to become associated with purely mundane passions, which often actually give it the character of sport. No one knows who will live in this cage in the future, or whether at the end of this tremendous development entirely new prophets will arise, or whether there will be a great rebirth of old ideas and ideals, or, if neither, mechanized petrification, embellished with a sort of convulsive self-importance. For of the last stage of this cultural development, it might well be truly said: "Specialists without spirit, sensualists without heart; this nullity imagines that it has attained a level of civilization never before achieved."[1]

Though Weber's caustic attack on the American culture was written nearly a century ago, many European and other critics of the United States and its cultural exports, from Disney to MTV, would repeat it today. What reply should Americans make?

Perhaps, in this age of worldwide striving for economic growth, affluence, higher productivity, better technology, mass consumption, and entertainment, Americans should reply, "You, too!" Indeed, the economic success of other capitalist countries, particularly of Japan, has led many Americans to worry that they are no longer capitalist enough.

What the free-market revolutionaries of the Republican Party say, however, is that far from spawning a dispirited, heartless society, American capitalism retains its religious and ethical meaning. "Our civilization is based on a spiritual and moral dimension," insists Newt Gingrich. "America is a series of romantic folktales that just happen to be true. We are a unique civilization. We stand on the shoulders of Western European civilization, but we are far more futuristic, more populist, and more inclusive." To be sure, the bottom line remains ... the bottom line: "The lesson of American civilization is that inventing new forms of wealth is the key to a better future."[2]

Of course, this embellished expression of the traditional American free-enterprise creed would not have surprised Weber in the least.

Free Enterprise v. Social Responsibilities

After World War II, the debate over American capitalism brought the devotees of free enterprise up against proponents of a newer "social responsibilities" doctrine. The free enterprisers held that the aim of business was and should be to maximize profits, within the rules of the game set by law.[3] In the words of one leading champion, "It is inconceivable to a one-hundred per cent American that anyone except a nut should give something for nothing."[4] Milton Friedman used more parliamentary language in his classic enunciation of postwar free-market, or laissez-faire, ideology, *Capitalism and Freedom:* "Few trends could so thoroughly undermine the very foundations of our free society as the acceptance by corporate officials of a social responsibility other than to make as much money for their stockholders as possible."[5]

Social-responsibilities advocates, by contrast, contended that this exclusive profit-maximizing philosophy had become an anachronism. It had made sense once upon a time, when business was struggling to win freedom from "tyrannical kings" and mercantilist control, but no longer in today's society, where huge corporations play social and political roles that go beyond the purely economic. Corporations cannot avoid having a conspicuous impact on society, which society either approves or opposes, permits or prevents. Hence, the advocates said, if business wants to retain its autonomy, it must be prepared to assume certain social responsibilities—and be willing to see government take on social functions that the market does not perform adequately.

In a word, business executives must seek to coordinate their company's and their own private aims with public purposes, as expressed through the political process. They could do this "and still be successful," asserted Thomas J. Watson, Jr., the late chairman of IBM, who nevertheless added: "I would be the first to admit that it's a good deal easier to state this proposition than to put it into practice. One of our most important continuing problems is the question of how we can strike a balance between what is sound business practice in the management of our large organizations and what is good for the national interest. It is a dilemma which will confront us more and more often in the years ahead."[6]

Business people in America have tended to oscillate between the two creeds, accepting social responsibilities and a larger governmental role in periods of crisis, while stressing the free-enterprise ideology in normal times or whenever it becomes necessary to fight the encroachment of government in their affairs. Virtually all, regardless of the times, insist that higher profits serve the broad public interest—by stimulating investment, accelerating economic growth, and creating more jobs.

To demonstrate their dedication to these worthy ends, corporate executives like to talk about the importance of maximizing long-term rather than short-term profits. In day-to-day business affairs, they say, decisions must sometimes be made that will in the short run cost the company something but in the long run will lead to its survival or growth.[7] Not infrequently, they extend this reasoning to corporate actions that will expand their markets, thereby helping to spur the national and international economy. One may doubt, however, that many business people have this sort of wide-ranging vision, as opposed to an ardent devotion to their own immediate interest. One prominent business-man, who insisted on anonymity, put it this way: "All businessmen, on the make, aim at short-term profit maximization. When they've risen in the world enough to behave like statesmen, they aim at long-run profit maximization. But the real truth—the truth that a businessman will tell only to his wife or best friend— is that he still aims at short-run profit maximization."[8]

Most of all, American business executives are determined not to appear softheaded. Whether partisans of free enterprise or social responsibilities, they generally deny that they ever behave altruistically, rather than out of, at most, enlightened self-interest. In this respect, they (and most of their compatriots) seem not to have changed at all since the 1830s, when a visiting Alexis de Tocqueville observed that "the doctrine of self-interest properly understood" had won universal acceptance among Americans— who, he thought, often failed to do themselves justice. Even though he found that they, like people everywhere, sometimes gave way to "the disinterested, spontaneous impulses natural to man," Tocqueville reported that the Americans "are hardly prepared to admit that they do give way to emotions of this sort. They prefer to give the credit to their philosophy rather than to themselves."[9] When, a century later, Americans helped rescue a war-devastated Europe with the Marshall Plan, they insisted they were only pursuing national self-interest or at best "mutual" interest, even as the recipients hailed the plan as an unprecedented act of national generosity. Paradoxically, many of the same hardheaded Americans were outraged by the failure of some Europeans to be more grateful for their professedly nonaltruistic behavior.

Limited Government

American "selfishness" is, in a sense, built into the origins of the republic. What entitled the colonists to cast off British rule was, as Thomas Jefferson explained in the Declaration of Independence, the fact that they were all "created equal" and endowed with the "unalienable Rights" of "Life, Liberty, and the pursuit of Happiness." That meant they could not be bound by the sovereign will of the English king to provide taxes for the common good of his majesty's empire. In the new country, the people would be sovereign and the government a limited thing, set up by the consent of the governed to protect their individual rights.

This was the essence of the American social contract, drawn up on the strength of over a century of philosophical theorizing in Europe and the Americans' own practical experience managing many of their affairs. Thus, responding to critics who accused him of plagiarism, Jefferson insisted that he had "aimed neither at originality of principle or sentiment" but at "an expression of the American mind." His words, he said, reflected "the harmonizing sentiments of the day, whether expressed in conversation, in letters, printed essays or in the elementary books of public right, such as Aristotle, Cicero, Locke . . . etc." [10]

The American social contract limited government to what the people *would* allow, but it did not say how much government the people *should* allow. In our own time, philosophers have used social-contract theory to justify everything from a full-fledged welfare state to minimalist libertarian government.[11] Historically, the extent to which the American social contract can legitimately be used to deal with the problems of a capitalist economy has been under debate since the Constitutional convention.

The early representatives of the opposing points of view were Jefferson himself, who believed in a weak central government, and Alexander Hamilton, who felt it should be strong and activist. As the economist Daniel W. Bromley has noted, Hamilton, the first secretary of the Treasury, "understood—long before

John Maynard Keynes offered decisive proof—that the national government must use its fiscal powers to promote certain critical sectors of the economy. While he was committed to the idea of markets, he saw them as an extension of the government's legislative and executive capacities."[12] Backed by President Washington and over Jefferson's opposition, Hamilton used the general-welfare clause of the Constitution in 1791 to justify creating the first Bank of the United States, which was upheld as constitutional by the Supreme Court in *McCulloch v. Maryland*. Two generations later, the Jeffersonian tradition reasserted itself when President Andrew Jackson vetoed a bill to keep the Second Bank of the United States in business past 1836.

In practice, Americans were not at all averse to government involvement in economic enterprise. Before the Civil War, state and local governments took a considerable hand in helping to build canals and railroads, among other things. From the 1860s on, the federal government expanded upon its relatively modest record of land donation and undertook to subsidize construction of the transcontinental railroads, make public lands in the West available to settlers, create the land-grant colleges, and finance science and technology. To be sure, economic expenditures by the federal government grew slowly. As late as 1929, total federal outlays amounted to only $1.3 billion—about 1 percent of gross national product that year. By comparison, state and local spending in 1929 totaled $7.2 billion. Before the federal government became a major player in the economy as a source of expenditures, however, it was being widely called upon to regulate business activity.

As the economic historian Jonathan Hughes has demonstrated, ideological and rhetorical enthusiasm for free enterprise has tended to obscure the fact that, thanks to the importation of

English common law, government regulation of economic life has been a constant part of the American scene from the beginning.[13] In colonial America, everything from land use to trade practices to wages and prices came under the regulatory control of the authorities, starting at the village level. Through the first three-quarters of the nineteenth century this habit of recourse to "nonmarket controls" continued to be exercised without letup by state and local governments. Then, starting around 1870, Washington began to assume responsibility for setting rules and standards for an economy increasingly dominated by large and powerful corporations.

Campaigning for his antitrust act in the 1880s, Republican Senator John Sherman of Ohio declared that "society is now disturbed by forces never felt before." If Congress refused to act, there would soon be "a trust for every production and a master to fix the price for every necessity of life." For his part, the industrialist Andrew Carnegie declared that mass production involved heavy fixed charges and that a chaotic market would wreck huge industries, cause capital to be wasted and depleted, and prevent national industrial development. The days of Adam Smith were dead and gone, said Carnegie. James B. Dill, the lawyer who brought Carnegie and J. P. Morgan together to form the U.S. Steel Corporation, told the reporter Lincoln Steffens: "Trusts are natural, inevitable growths out of our social and economic conditions. You cannot stop them by force, with laws. They will sweep down like glaciers upon your police, courts, and States and wash them into flowing rivers. I am clearing the way for them."[14]

Nevertheless, trusts were broken up—in the name of preserving free competition in open markets. Even more significantly, the electoral success of agrarian populists and urban progressives resulted in the creation of a host of federal laws and agencies to limit the power of capitalist enterprise. By World War I, interstate commerce (the railroads), mining, trade practices, and the food and drug industry had come under federal supervision. With the creation of the Federal Reserve System, a central banking authority was established for the first time since Andrew Jackson's day. For the first time ever, a system of land conservation was created by way of national parks and forests. Efforts were also made to regulate hours, wages, working conditions, and child labor. Passage of the Sixteenth Amendment in 1913 permitted the accumulation of personal wealth itself to be regulated by way of a graduated income tax. As Hughes notes, "Control gained the upper hand over the new laissez-faire at the federal level because powerful groups rejected the decision of the free market regarding the ownership and distribution of economic power." [15]

The advance of the new federal regulatory regime was interrupted during the 1920s, during which a series of Republican administrations hearkened to a revival of free-market ideology. But then came the Great Depression. On the eve of the November, 1932, election, President Herbert Hoover saw something coming, and feared it. "My countrymen," he declared, "the proposals of our opponents represent a profound change in American life—less in concrete proposal, bad as that may be, than by implication and evasion. Dominantly in their spirit, they represent a radical departure from the foundations of 150 years which have made this the greatest nation in the world. This election is not a mere shift from the ins to the outs. It means deciding the direction our Nation will take over a century to come." [16]

As Hoover had foreseen, the election of Franklin Delano Roosevelt did bring about a profound change in the economic role of the United States government. Some of the New Deal programs, like the Works Progress Administration and the Public Works Administration, were emergency measures that soon vanished. But other initiatives became a permanent part of the American system, such as the Social Security pensions, unemployment compensation, public welfare, the Federal Deposit Insurance Corporation, the Home Loan Bank Board, the Securities and Exchange Commission, the Agricultural Adjustment Act, the Fair Labor Standards Act, and the National Labor Relations Board. Most of these programs built on earlier precedents. (Social Security, for example, built on a tradition of federal support for widows and orphans that began with the payment of Civil War pensions.) But taken together, they meant that for the first time the federal government was assuming responsibility for maintaining a satisfactory level of economic life.[17] Hughes sees the culmination of this new approach in the Employment Act of 1946, which officially made economic growth an aim of national public policy.

By expanding government's role in rescuing the victims of the Depression, the New Deal saved American capitalism. In 1933, the year it was launched, Hitler took power in Germany and installed his National Socialist regime. In effect, the United States government kept its side of the social contract by protecting the people's rights to life, liberty, and pursuit of happiness in the face of economic conditions that threatened to take them away. It was not, in Friedrich von Hayek's words, "the road to serfdom." On the contrary, it preserved political and economic freedom and barred the way to the totalitarian revolutions that some Americans, like Charles and Anne Lindbergh, thought were "the wave of the future." Even Herbert Hoover paid a visit to Hitler in 1938 to assure him that Americans considered not Nazism but communism the real enemy.

The fundamental New Deal reforms of the American system survived for decades under both Democratic and Republican administrations. Lyndon Johnson's Great Society built upon and expanded them, through efforts to wipe out poverty and to extend medical assistance to the aged and disabled. After the 1970 elections, Richard Nixon declared, "I am now a Keynesian," and as if to prove his emancipation from laissez faire, on August 15, 1971, announced a New Economic Policy that froze wages, prices, and rents; devalued the dollar and suspended its convertibility into gold; imposed a surtax on imports; and cut taxes. For a president and a party that had heretofore always sworn by free enterprise, it seemed like a wholesale conversion to the ideology of federal economic management.[18]

Nevertheless, the New Deal tide was beginning to turn. Nixon himself took steps to return federal dollars to the states in the form of block grants. Gerald Ford and the next Democratic president, Jimmy Carter, commenced deregulating airline service and interstate commerce, areas in which the regulators were widely recognized as having been captured by the regulated, to the detriment of consumers. And then came the first major attempt to reverse the economic role of the United States government.

The Reagan Play

The 1980 presidential campaign of Ronald Reagan was powered by two different types of conservatives. One was a group of "populists" of the right, whose main goal was to slash taxes—in the spirit of California's Proposition 13 tax revolt. This group of conservatives was dominated by small and medium-sized business people, small-town bankers, savings and loan operators, real estate dealers, homeowners, farmers, white-collar and even many blue-collar workers worried about their jobs. They saw themselves as "middle Americans," and they showed scant sympathy for those below them (especially blacks and those on welfare), and little, either, for big business.

The other group included many of those very representatives of big business and big banking who had earlier distanced themselves from Reagan as a right-wing populist, the foe of the moderate and predominantly Eastern Establishment wing of the Republican Party. The thinking of these business-establishment conservatives was focused on the importance of checking inflation, especially by monetary policy, and on stimulating savings and corporate investment, preserving the international economic and monetary system, balancing the budget, and breaking the power of organized labor.

Reagan's philosophy was an amalgam of these two conservative creeds, wrapped together with traditional American boosterism: "It's morning in America!" If free enterprise could be liberated from the heavy hand of government controls and the pressures of organized labor, America would soon regain its powerful economic momentum and its global dominance. Inflation would be stopped by slowing the rate of monetary growth and breaking the power of labor to raise wages faster than productivity; and economic growth would be accelerated by slashing taxes. Reagan's supply-side economic counsellors, headed by David Stockman, a former Michigan Congressman, produced a paper called "On the Danger of a GOP Economic Dunkirk," which was leaked to *The New York Times*. It urged the new president to tell Congress and the nation that "the economic, financial, budget, and regulatory conditions he inherited are far worse than anyone had imagined." A Reagan Revolution was needed to save the nation.

On taking office, Reagan began to move against the New Deal revision of the social contract. One sign of his determination was his firing of 11,400 members of the Professional Air Traffic Controllers Organization, a union of government workers, for participating in an illegal strike. Another major act was the weakening of financial and antitrust regulation, which unleashed a boom in mergers and acquisitions, corporate buyouts, and managerial stock buybacks, together with the highly speculative growth of savings and loan (S & L) institutions, banks, and real estate investment, much of it financed by junk bonds and a rapid increase in corporate debt.[19]

The S&L bankruptcies added up to the biggest financial scandal in American history, possibly costing over one trillion dollars. A looting frenzy brought on by corruption, it was also an ideological setback for the true believers in what Reagan called "the magic of the market." Even L. William Seidman, a Reagan admirer and conservative free-enterpriser who headed the Federal Deposit Insurance Corporation, blamed the ideologues for careless and excessive deregulation—for forgetting that the government's loose use of its "full faith and credit had castrated the market's regulatory strength" and had created "an open invitation to gamble with other people's money."[20]

The deregulation of banking and finance and the debt explosion and takeover wave contributed little to the nation's economic growth. What they brought was a great deal of corporate downsizing and layoffs of both workers and managers. The business personalities most likely to be remembered as the non-heroes of the Reagan Revolution are the financial wheeler-dealers Charles Keating, chairman of Lincoln Savings and Loan, and Michael Milken, junk-bond king of Drexel Burnham Lambert, both of whom went to jail.

Along with the explosion of private debt came a quadrupling of the public debt during the Reagan-Bush years. Reagan's anti-government ideology made him a ready convert to the "supply-side" economics of such advisers as Arthur Laffer of the University of California, Jude Wanniski, a former editorial writer on *The Wall Street Journal*, Representative Jack Kemp of upstate New York, Senator William V. Roth of Delaware, as well as David Stockman, who, as the administration's budget director, came to be known as the "Robespierre of the Reagan Revolution." At their urging, Reagan threw his full support behind the Kemp-Roth bill for cutting personal income tax rates by 30 percent, accepting the theory, embodied in the so-called "Laffer Curve," that the tax cut would so energize managers and workers that it would increase national economic growth enough to generate tax revenues that would cover, or more than cover, the huge tax cuts. The deficit, therefore, would be no problem, and over time it would shrink.

Nothing like that happened. Instead, the federal debt, which had not quite reached $1 trillion when Reagan took office, more than tripled during his eight-year term. Coached by his intellectual advisers—not only the supply-siders but Milton Friedman, the conservative monetarist and Nobel laureate—Reagan came to regard the deficit as a positive good: a barrier to government spending programs.

Was it all a hoax, designed to serve the interests of the rich? Stockman's most famous, or infamous, remark, to William Greider, then of the *Washington Post*, was that the big tax cut was a "Trojan Horse." Without deep cuts in government spending, the deficits would soar. But there would be no deep spending cuts. On the contrary, Reagan himself, with the backing of Congress, stood for a big military buildup and neither he nor Con-

gress would chop Social Security and other major federal programs, for which there was still strong public support.

"By 1982," Stockman later wrote, "I knew the Reagan Revolution was impossible—it was a metaphor with no anchor in
political and economic reality . . . I never gave up the supply-
side ideology, however. I just put it in my safe, along with other
intellectual valuables. It was simply not operationally relevant in
the world of democratic fact where the politicians have the last
and final say." So, unable to beat them, Stockman joined the
politicians—though, he said, "I couldn't stand the idea of making all those deals to preserve their booty and waste." In the end,
he concluded, "There has been no Reagan Revolution."[21]

But there really was a Reagan Revolution—an anti-tax, red
ink, deregulatory, government-inhibiting revolution—that
would cast a long shadow over the American economy and set
the stage for the Republican takeover of Congress in 1994. It left
the United States with a tattered social contract and a deeply
unbalanced budget that severely restricted the ability of the federal government to deal with the new and vexing problems
troubling the United States and the rest of the world in the post-
communist era.

The most enduring legacy of the Reagan years has been a
heightened public resistance to paying taxes. Most Americans
now appear to regard taxation not as "the price of civilization"
but as a rip-off by politicians and bureaucrats of their hard-
earned money for the benefit of those who like to feed at the
public trough. (Of course, the privileged are generally reluctant
to surrender their own place at the trough, as are members of the
vast middle class, who are happy to have Social Security, Medicare, and various other public retirement programs, but unhappy
about paying for them.) No single action hurt George Bush polit-

ically more than reneging on his ill-advised pledge ("Read my lips") not to raise taxes. Implicitly acknowledging the Reagan administration's preferential option for the rich with his promise of a "kinder, gentler America," Bush equivocated between appealing to centrist voters and kowtowing to the Republican right, ultimately pleasing no one.

In the first two years of his presidential term, Bill Clinton sought to undo the legacy of the Reagan-Bush years by raising taxes and restraining the growth of total outlays, military and civilian, to shrink the deficit; by trying to bring corporate executives and labor leaders together in an effort to create more jobs and increase productive efficiency; by expanding aid for the working poor through larger tax credits; and by restoring financial regulation and antitrust enforcement. He even initiated a significant effort to shrink the size of the federal workforce. But his image as a "New Democrat" was badly tarnished by his disastrously unsuccessful attempt to reform the nation's health care system.

The Clinton plan, which sought to guarantee medical coverage for all Americans by way of large "user groups" and managed health care, was a far cry from the government-run medical programs of other Western nations. But Republicans and business interests opposed to any new federal mandates successfully portrayed it as a huge government intrusion on peoples' freedom of choice. Indeed, some Republican partisans resisted any extension of federal health care guarantees not because they wouldn't work but on the purely ideological grounds that passage would undermine public opposition to all government-sponsored solutions to social problems. William Kristol, former chief of staff to Vice President Dan Quayle and a leading Republican intellectual strategist, put it this way in a 1993 memo urging that the

Clinton plan be killed rather than amended: "It will relegitimize middle-class dependence for 'security' on government spending and regulation. It will revive the reputation of the party that spends and regulates, the Democrats, as the generous protector of middle-class interests. And it will at the same time strike a punishing blow against Republican claims to defend the middle class by restraining government."[22] The demise of the Clinton health care plan was the beginning of the 1994 Republican ascendancy.

The New Laissez-Faire

The Republicans who took control of the House of Representatives in January, 1995, were not exaggerating when they called themselves revolutionaries. In the course of the year, House leaders, with the strong backing of seventy-three enthusiastic Republican freshmen, proved by legislative effort and public pronouncement that they wanted not merely to reduce the size of the federal government but fundamentally to alter its role in the American system.

The extent of the revolution was only partly visible in the G.O.P.'s Contract with America, which was less an anti-government program than a catch-all conservative political platform designed to appeal to voters while generating a minimum of controversy. Getting tougher on crime, reducing product liability lawsuits, setting Congressional term limits, requiring Congress to comply with workplace and civil rights laws, prohibiting further cuts in the defense budget—these had nothing to do with shrinking the federal government or changing its role. The balanced budget amendment to the Constitution (which failed by one vote in the Senate) and the presidential line-item veto could facilitate but would not necessitate a reduction of federal expenditures. The proposal to reduce federal paperwork and restrict so-called unfunded mandates was sufficiently uncontroversial to win quick approval from both houses and be signed into law by President Clinton. But the Contract's welfare plan and its package of $350 billion in tax cuts over seven years (later reduced to $245 billion by compromise with the Senate leadership) clearly indicated a radical shift of direction.

The welfare plan (a version of which President Clinton signed into law in the summer of 1996) aimed at ending the federal government's sixty-year guarantee of assistance to all single mothers with dependent children. Passing both the House and Senate by large margins, it limited such aid to a maximum of five years per recipient while sharply reducing the projected federal welfare contribution; it would be transformed into block grants which the states would have wide latitude to use as they saw fit. The tax-cut package, when combined with a resolution to balance the federal budget by the year 2002 (passed after the budget-balancing amendment failed) and the refusal to reduce defense expenditures, meant that domestic spending would have to undergo a real reduction of 30 percent. To meet that goal, the Republicans proceeded to take their cleaver not only to discretionary spending programs but to entitlements, including $270 billion from health care for the elderly and disabled (Medicare) and $182 billion from health care for the poor (Medicaid). A number of federal programs and agencies were slated for the dustheap, including the Commerce Department, around since the days of Theodore Roosevelt; and there were plans to privatize some IRS collections and sell off public lands and national parks.

The Republicans also set out to enfeeble federal regulatory

power both through changes in regulation and budget cuts of 30 percent and more in agencies such as the Food and Drug Administration, the Occupational Safety and Health Administration, and the Environmental Protection Agency. Efforts were mounted to weaken clean air and water standards, relax controls on pesticides, and cease requiring polluters to clean up their waste. The FDA's authority to guarantee the effectiveness of drugs came under attack; as long as the supposed remedy was not positively harmful, let the buyer beware and the market decide.

For starters, the Republican program represented an effort to erase the New Deal assumption that the federal government has a responsibility for providing a measure of economic security for individuals and the country at large. No longer was there talk about maintaining a social "safety net" for the poor. The bulk of the tax relief, which included a long-sought cut in the capital gains tax, would go to the wealthy. Meanwhile, those at the lower end of society would see cutbacks not only in welfare and health care but in public housing and legal representation. The working poor would lose a portion of the earned income tax credit, by which the government lifted them above the poverty line. In the name of reducing "corporate welfare," the Republicans also proposed to axe the tax-credit program that provided private and nonprofit developers with market-based incentives to build low-income housing. Much Republican rhetoric stressed how all such programs did the poor more harm than good, robbed them of their dignity, undermined private charity, and so forth. But there was little effort to hide the harder edges: Any programs that transferred wealth from haves to have-nots were "redistributionist," and as such had to go.

Meanwhile, the assault on federal regulatory authority offered a vision of unfettered capitalism in which individual liberty is the highest good and free markets are always preferable to government intervention. This vision was hardly new, but since the late 1970s it had acquired precise shape in the white papers and policy proposals generated by a group of conservative think tanks and foundations, including the Heritage Foundation, the Cato Institute, the Bradley Foundation, the Scaife Foundation, and the Ethics and Public Policy Foundation. A new laissez-faire intelligentsia had sprung into being, some of whom went so far as to oppose the use of language that even hinted at the communitarian ideals of the welfare state. Thus, David Frum, in his book *Dead Right*, took to task William Bennett, the former Education secretary and drug czar, for titling his 1992 book *The De-valuing of America: The Struggle for Our Children and Our Culture.* "What," asked Frum,

> is the locution "our children" doing in Bennett's mouth? The phrase contains the thought that one's obligations to all the other children in the country are similar in nature to one's obligations to one's own; that a purely political bond—that between citizens of one nation—can resemble in some meaningful way the biological bond between parent and child. For people who are always trying to extend the reach of the political, this is an attractive claim to make.[23]

Such hostility to the very concept of a political community meant that even democratic government was at best a necessary evil— necessary to protect individual rights but evil because it imposed the will of majorities on unwilling minorities. In the words of the Cato Institute's Constitutional expert, Roger Pilon, "[W]hile majoritarian democracy may be preferable to other forms of rule in that it enables the ruled to participate in the decisionmaking process, in the end it is simply a process through which to decide, not a process that imparts legitimacy to the decisions that follow."[24]

This anti-government vision extended from the libertarian think tanks to the Christian Right, where evangelical and "Reconstructionist" writers called efforts to "macro-manage" the economy "unbiblical" and pronounced all taxes other than a poll tax "ungodly." According to these writers, the state had no role to play beyond providing for the common defense and insuring justice—which, to be sure, extended to enforcing "biblical" moral standards. But virtually all forms of government economic regulation were disallowed, including minimum wage laws, restrictions on advertising, licensing of the professions, and zoning laws.[25] As extreme as these positions might seem, it is notable that only slightly less radical worldviews were laid out in books published in 1995 by the two leaders of the Republican Revolution: former political science professor Newt Gingrich and former economics professor Dick Armey.

Gingrich, an enthusiast of the futuristic imaginings of Alvin and Heidi Toffler, urged Americans to reject the "calculated effort by cultural elites" to discredit American civilization and "accelerate America's entry into the Third Wave Information Age." Regulation, litigation, taxation, public education, welfare, the structure of our government bureaucracies—these were all products of the Industrial Age, whose time had now passed. In Gingrich's view, if America were to remain the predominant economy in the new global marketplace it would have to go back to the future: "While the Industrial Revolution herded people into gigantic social institutions—big corporations, big unions, big government—the Information Revolution is breaking up these giants and leading us back to something that is— strangely enough—much more like de Tocqueville's 1830s

America." As in the country's nominally laissez-faire heyday, the new Information Age would, he claimed, "be a bit like rafting down the rapids after we have learned to canoe on a quiet lake." If some of us happened to fall overboard, that presumably was a price worth paying for the exhilaration of the new economic environment.[26]

Armey, with a cast of mind more spiritual than sci-fi, did not justify his anti-government philosophy in terms of American competitiveness. He portrayed free enterprise as a calling from God, and opposed government intervention in the economy on principle, even should it prove efficacious. "Liberals," he wrote, "keep coming up with their schemes for collective progress, which makes them seem positive and hopeful. In our view these plans are generally hare-brained, which makes us seem negative. But if they did work they would insult the dignity of a free people."[27] To be sure, he tiptoed around certain federal guarantees, contenting himself merely with pointing out the cost of laws that insure bank deposits, pensions, and loans. And he made no mention of unemployment insurance or emergency disaster relief, which by his lights would seem to be an unwarranted government retardation of the automatic adjustment mechanism of the free market. His great love, which he hoped to realize in phase two of the revolution, was an ungraduated, or flat, income tax; indeed, when millionaire publisher Steve Forbes's flat-tax plan foundered in the early rounds of the 1996 presidential campaign, Armey rushed up to New Hampshire to defend the concept.

In Gingrich, Armey, and their intellectual cohorts, it was not easy to discover any acknowledgment that laissez-faire capitalism might ever create undesirable results, whether environmental pollution, monopolies, a shortage of consumer information and protection, or economic downturns. Gingrich, maintaining his boyhood interest in natural history, did offer a few kind words for protecting endangered species. More characteristic, however, was his claim that "[t]he so-called business cycle is in large part a product of the theories of American economists." [28] What he appeared to mean by this was that the Federal Reserve Board creates recessions by acting to prevent inflation in times of economic growth. How this would explain the recurrent recessions and depressions of the late nineteenth century, when there was no central bank, he neglected to mention. Mostly the Speaker of the House appeared to be reflecting the traditional small-business desire for easy money.

Without venturing an opinion on the causes of the business cycle, Armey, too, made clear his opposition to federal economic intervention. In his version of recent American economic history, the onetime economics professor applauded Ronald Reagan for sending "the big thinkers" packing when he took office: "No more macroeconomic meddling. No more talk of aggregates this and aggregates that. Above all, no more reliance upon 'experts,' but instead a reliance on real men and women." Looking to a brave new Republican future, Armey asked (rhetorically) who would "'manage the economy,' subsidize the needy, regulate industry, and do all the things Washington does today?" The answer: "The people themselves, individually and through their local representatives. This is how a free country works." [29] Evidently, in Armeynomics, there was no place for countercyclical fiscal or monetary policy—raising or lowering taxes, shrinking or expanding the money supply—in order to keep the economy on track.

Antitrust? Armey celebrated the thousands of small computer software companies that, between 1975 and 1985, competed against one another to create a new world information order that no large corporation could have imagined. But he betrayed no concern that by the 1990s, a large number of them had been gobbled up by the Microsoft corporation. Was he, unlike Theodore Roosevelt and William Howard Taft, unconcerned about the effect of monopolies on the free enterprise system? Or was he just ideologically opposed to the federal government getting involved? "Who," he asked, "except a few social levelers in the Clinton Justice Department begrudges Bill Gates, the founder of Microsoft, his billions?" A Baptist, Armey acknowledged that money was not the "end-all of human existence." But he recast Jesus's injunction that "it is easier for a camel to go through the eye of a needle than for a rich man to enter into the kingdom of God," to mean merely that "wealth alone" will not get you into heaven.[30]

By the end of 1995, it was clear that the House Republicans had seriously overestimated their ability to take the country by legislative storm. Opinion polls and Democratic successes in the November off-year elections left no doubt that the American public had become scared by all the talk of revolution, whether it concerned weakening federal commitments to environmental protection or to the social safety net. Emboldened, President Clinton vetoed bills that would have made sweeping changes in Medicare and Medicaid. He also vetoed a balanced-budget bill, and when Republicans tried to force his hand by linking it to approval of a rise in the debt ceiling, he twice let the government shut down rather than give in. The final 1996 budget, which did not pass until April, fell far short of the G.O.P.'s 1995 aims; although there were significant cuts in discretionary domestic spending, nearly all the agencies and regulatory regimes targeted for extinction survived.

Even Republican voters seemed uncertain about which way to turn. In the G.O.P. primary campaign, talk of the Contract with America all but disappeared after the Iowa caucuses, when Texas Senator Phil Gramm dropped out of the race. Meanwhile, Forbes offered up unreconstructed Reagan-era supply-side economics—shunning all talk of hard, budget-balancing decisions—while Pat Buchanan rallied his troops by rejecting free-trade orthodoxy and assailing corporate America for laying off workers. With his unabashed enthusiasm for stoking the fires of nativism and his appeals to God and family, Buchanan offered an almost pre-capitalist image of the future completely at odds with the Freedom Revolution that had dominated Capitol Hill the year before.

The uncertain course of the new laissez-faire only emphasized the openness of fundamental questions about the nature of the capitalist system. How much regulation do advanced technological economies require? What steps should government take to protect the people from hard times? How far do such protections inhibit a country's ability to compete in the world's markets? Unlike the physical sciences, human societies never offer the opportunity for perfectly controlled experiments. But as they wrestled with the questions, Americans had an unprecedented opportunity to compare the claims of Gingrichian free-marketers, Buchananite protectionists, Clintonian neoliberals, and the rest with capitalist experimentation taking place all over the world. From the troubled efforts of reformers to transform the former Soviet bloc into healthy market economies to an economically thriving but politically repressive China, from a Japan trying to decide how far to liberalize its markets to a Northern Europe struggling with unwinding its welfare states, there were insights to be gleaned, lessons to be learned.

FOUR

∙∙

The Soviet Bloc in Transition

Bernard Wasow*

I n the face of steady decline in popular support for reform in the Former Soviet Bloc (FSB), a set of stories has come into circulation about economic change there. In this conventional wisdom, the debate between "Gradualism" vs. "Big Bang" was won by reformers in Russia and in most of Eastern Europe; decisive reform, continued against considerable opposition, has borne fruit; much of Eastern Europe is growing vigorously and Russia is expected to show positive growth very soon; even laggards—Ukraine and the Asian republics—are haltingly pledging to do the right thing: stabilize, liberalize, and privatize their economies.

*In addition to extensive travel and work in the Third World, the author taught economics at the Central European University in Prague in the autumn of 1992 and participated in two World Bank missions to Mongolia in 1994. This chapter was written when he was an Associate Professor of Economics at New York University and a consultant to the Twentieth Century Fund. It represents his views alone.

There is reason to doubt these stories. Contrary to what many in the West believe, the economic crisis of most of the FSB is not moving steadily toward resolution. Political setbacks in the FSB are not anomalous stumbles on the road to capitalism but a direct result of failed reform. While a booming service economy and exploding wealth for a narrow elite provide surface glitter, little has been done to solve the fundamental economic problem of making industry and agriculture healthy and productive. Little has been done to remove the conditions that lead governments to monetary profligacy. Altogether, more than half a decade after the transition began, most of the FSB is still in a deep economic mess.

No successful Big Bang has taken place. Indeed, no credible economic "shock therapy" has been applied. Repeatedly, FSB governments have agreed to radical reforms, and then proceeded with the most halting of half-measures. The governments have moved gradually—most of them incoherently and ad hoc, a few, like the Czech Republic and Estonia, more successfully. Nevertheless, Russia's success compared to Ukraine is routinely attributed to its adherence to "shock therapy."[1] In Russia, a period of shock therapy did occur for a few months, from January until April or May of 1992, under Boris Yeltsin and his chief economic reformer, Yegor Gaidar. But since then, the old Soviet managers and bureaucrats have succeeded in protecting their vested interests very well.[2] Government hiring binges have added thousands of employees to the public sector.[3] This may have been an understandable political response to the threat of growing unemployment, but it is part of no coherent "therapy."

If early reformers of the FSB had no idea how rough were the waters that needed to be crossed, neither did Western advisers understand what they were up against. As the crisis persisted, little advice and less financial aid were directed to helping people who had only vague ideas about their destination solve the political challenges of getting there.

The Real Story

As the Soviet empire disintegrated in 1989 and 1990, Karl Marx and V. I. Lenin were supplanted in the Russian pantheon of Great Men by such icons of the free market as Friedrich von Hayek and Milton Friedman. Russians who pursued the study of Western economics, and there were many, found the prospect of open financial markets, most of all stock markets, immensely fascinating. After a long day of studying the mundane core of Western economic theory, eager students asked Western teachers for more relevant material: How could one decode the financial pages of the *Wall Street Journal?* Surely it was in these arcane columns that one could find the keys to prosperity. Wasn't the wealth of the West brewed in the cauldrons of high finance? Homilies about efficient production and compound productivity growth at single digit rates could hardly satisfy people who were straining to enjoy the cornucopia of the market.

In Russia, as in countries from Romania to Mongolia, hucksters of every sort sold opportunities to get rich quick. Weren't quick riches what capitalism was all about? But instead of Professor Friedman, whose portraits and quotes took pride of place in many a formerly communist office, Charles Ponzi would have been a better emblem of the spirit of free markets in the Wild East.

Almost no one in the FSB appreciated the true economic situation. Russia and its allies were not advanced industrial societies that, with the addition of efficient financial markets, would provide all the goods and services enjoyed by Westerners. They were grossly distorted economies that could not survive in world markets without radical surgery. Many of their huge factories added little or no value to the materials they processed. The services they provided their employees—from housing to day care to summer holidays—were financed by a surplus that could only exist in a price regime that all but gave away energy and raw materials.

In contrast to the feelings of triumph and hope that accompanied the end of communist totalitarianism, the FSB in 1990 was anything but a land that had managed to win a war without a single great battle. Economically, it was more like a defeated country with its factories and farms in ruins. But who could be expected to recognize the devastation? Unlike Germany in 1945, the rubble of war was not piled all around. In the FSB, the factories were in place and the workers were ready to file in. The fields were ready to be plowed in the spring and harvested in the fall.

In reality, however, most units of production were incapable of survival if that meant purchasing inputs and selling output in international competition. Firms depended on inputs at concessionary prices and a flow of unrepayable credits. Efficient financial markets, privatization, and most of all free, untaxed, and unsubsidized competition from abroad would have been as helpful as smashing the windows of an overheated greenhouse on a winter's day. Nor was the fundamental economic problem to help existing firms adjust to new economic conditions. The units were too big. They were not economically located. Much of the machinery was good for nothing more than scrap metal. The economic structure was populated mostly by economic zombies, the living dead. They had to be removed and replaced, not rehabilitated. Had many of the factories and farms of the FSB been physically destroyed, the challenge might have been made not more difficult but easier.

A fundamental barrier to understanding economic reality in the FSB is that there is so little good information. To be sure, the World Bank, the International Monetary Fund (IMF), and other international agencies are producing data that are harmonized in format and presentation with data about other countries of the world. This provides, for example, detailed evidence to support the assertion that Gross Domestic Product (GDP) in Russia finally has begun to increase after five straight years of decline. But in fact, we have only the vaguest idea of aggregate economic performance in most of the FSB. Estimates of the decline of Russian GDP between 1991 and 1994, for example, have ranged from 20 percent to 50 percent. In its first survey of the Russian economy, the OECD noted that a major difficulty was to acquire the necessary policy information and statistical data.

The problem is not simply one of new concepts and scarce or incompetent staff.[4] There are capable people in state statistical bureaus in the FSB, but they have neither the power nor the ability to assemble good data. In the old days, economic accounting was a close partner to economic planning; however, there was no need and therefore no method for estimating most private sector production and investment activity. Now that economic planning has ceased to exist, there are in most places no methods, no procedures, and no enforceable reporting rules for obtaining accurate information from decentralized production units. Even state-owned firms may limit state access to "proprietary" data of the kind that every OECD government requires any private business to provide. Firms in the FSB are likely to try to hide as much information as they can from potential rivals and tax collectors; in many countries, they can hide most of it. The data that are assembled consist largely of official records from large state enterprises—something like counting fish caught in a net that once spanned the river but that now captures less and less of the flow. Missing are data on new service enterprises, successful private enterprises, and production that "falls off a truck."

Official statistics show economic recovery in most of the FSB beginning in the mid-1990s. Some recovery certainly is under-way; but the amount of off-the-book activity in even old firms renders most published reports highly suspect. Meanwhile, the estimates on which the international agencies base their aggre-gate statistics are driven by pressure within the IMF and the World Bank to find evidence of turnaround. The wishful data are needed for public relations campaigns to convince skeptical local bureaucrats that the painful adjustment program is working. Nobody is crudely fabricating numbers, though hopelessly ob-scure numbers—private investment in services, for example— may be produced by a visiting IMF expert from essentially whole cloth. The estimate may be better than nothing, but it's not much better.

Against the determinedly optimistic reports that prosperity is just around the corner, survey data suggest that the economic nadir has not yet been passed. The Open Media Research Insti-tute of Prague reported that barely half of all Poles considered themselves better off in 1995 than a year earlier, in an economy that reportedly had been growing robustly for two years.[5] The situation was worse in the Czech Republic and Estonia, two other stars of the transition. In Russia, Ukraine, and Belarus, fewer than 10 percent of the citizenry believed that their standard of living improved from 1994 to 1995. Such numbers are not incompatible with aggregate growth, but they undermine the notion that conditions are improving anywhere in the FSB for the average citizen. And they are supported by some frightening data on public health (though this information, too, is surely imperfect). Between 1991 and 1994, life expectancy for Russian men fell by eight years (to 57.3 years, below India's); between 1990 and 1994, infant mortality rose by more than 12 percent. The turbulence and uncertainty of life in Russia is reflected by the fact that in every one of its seventy-nine regional districts in 1994, birth rates were lower than death rates.[6]

General skepticism about recovery should not be taken to mean that everyone is suffering during the transition. One reason for the demise of industry in the FSB is that the raw materials and energy that local firms had consumed are so valuable. Export of raw and semiprocessed materials, arbitrage of energy price distortions, and the establishment of productive service enterprises have created wealth that is evident on the streets of capital cities throughout the FSB. But for the ordinary worker in the ordinary factory, the transition has not yet turned the corner. The task is not simply to raise aggregate value added, which can be accomplished simply by closing down activities that subtract value. It is to create, within an open, civil society, an economy with widespread opportunity for productive employment.

The Task of Transformation

The economic chaos that evolved from Gorbachev's initially modest efforts to restructure the economy came as a shock not only to Russian experts but to Westerners as well. The latter knew that a market economy could not function if managers were not accountable and if they had to respond to arbitrary prices. That was the reason advisers prescribed privatization and price liberalization. But a market system will also fail if managers neither understand the present value of their firms nor think of wealth- or profit-maximization as their primary task. And there can be *no* market economy if government aims to preserve existing institutions regardless of their ability to compete, while opportunists set about looting them.

The FSB's transition to a market economy involved more than reforming prices and ownership on the micro level and preserving monetary control on the macro level. The structure of social obligations and expectations had to change. Enterprise managers were pushed to assume daunting new roles: They had to decide what to produce and how to produce it—and find buyers once it had been produced. Extensive obligations to their workers such as housing, day care, and social activities remained a source of pride, but there now were also luxuries that reduced profits.

Under socialism, firms did not go bankrupt because their costs were too high or their products too shoddy. Workers did not lose their jobs or benefits because they performed poorly or because firms needed to economize. To be sure, money did some talking. There were black markets for goods and services, and professional fixers who for the right price could solve firms' problems. But these operated at the fringes of decent society. Not solid citizens but "opportunists" and "profiteers" made the deals and arbitraged the prices. Prices and profits did not determine which firms could expand; planners did. Prices did not decide which consumers received scarce goods and services; political connections and waiting on line did.

The monumental coordination problem of central planning was solved in part by simplification. Decisions about what would be produced and how were centralized. The number of firms was reduced. A firm in a market economy is the scene of thousands of decisions concerning the source of inputs, the technology of production, the markets in which to sell output, the pricing strategy, and the plans of investment. If one firm changes its decisions, many other firms are affected through what they buy and sell in markets. Prices play the central role in coordinating decisions among interconnected firms. As a price change modifies its costs, revenues, and profits, the enterprise will decide how to adjust its production plans profitably.

In the Soviet Union, quantitative goals for products and inputs use were set by planners and enforced by Communist Party functionaries. The problem of making firms' production plans roughly consistent with one another and then overseeing their realization was made manageable by reducing the number of plants—a strategy reinforced by the assumption that big plants were technically superior to small plants. In the defense sector, for example, there were approximately one hundred enterprises with ten thousand or more employees and no more than fifty plants with fewer than a thousand employees. The largest enterprises employed more than thirty thousand workers each. In the United States, by contrast, not a single establishment in the defense sector employs as many as ten thousand workers while hundreds of defense firms each employ fewer than one thousand.[7] The gigantic Soviet factories were spread around the country out of a concern for regional fairness. A huge plant in a relatively small city might be not simply the major employer but the only significant employer. According to one estimate, seventy towns and small cities in Russia each depended on a single defense establishment.[8]

So planners needed to coordinate the output of relatively few, massive plants, often located far from important producers of their inputs and users of their products. Even with relatively few very large firms, the planning problem was formidable. In addition to production within the former Soviet Union, international production needed to be coordinated. From Mongolia to Poland to Bulgaria, the members of the Soviet bloc (also known as Council of Mutual Economic Assistance), each with its own giant firms, planned international exchange of goods.

The problems that would bedevil the transition extended into each production unit. The Soviet educational system gave good fundamental training, but technicians' knowledge often was out of date and neither managers nor engineers had an adequate regard for cost. Outside of military and scientific applications, production technology seldom reflected the state of the art, even in the Third World. For example, while textile looms in Mexico and Colombia moved as fast as those in Western Europe—224 picks per minute (ppm)—Polish looms were running at 190 ppm and Mongolian looms at less than 150 ppm.[9]

The greatest competitive handicap facing industries seeking to make the transition has been their dependence on heavily subsidized energy. Even accounting for the exceptionally large size of their industrial sectors, the FSB (and China) used three times as much energy per capita in 1991 as other economies of similar income level.[10] In 1992, the energy subsidy in Russia was roughly the size of the entire GDP! Although energy prices were doubled the following year, that only brought them up to 30 percent of world levels.[11]

The FSB's international trading regime collapsed almost as soon as the Soviet Union itself did. To survive economically, managers had to find inputs and, more difficult, buyers for output. Although the prospect of supplying traditional customers remained attractive, each firm wanted to find better, cheaper inputs and each consumer wanted to buy better, cheaper products. Industrial production in the FSB collapsed because it was simply impossible to compete with the exporters of raw materials and importers of foreign goods.[12]

Even had plants been of optimum size, using cost-minimizing technology in ideal locations, manufacturing in the Soviet bloc probably would have been in deep trouble after the collapse of the socialist system. The Soviet conviction that manufacturing was productive and most services were not resulted in economies with overdeveloped industrial and stunted service sectors compared to market economies; there was simply more industrial output than a market economy could sustain. Other than countries heavily dependent on petroleum and other minerals, no market economy was as heavily industrialized as the communist countries, including the rapidly industrializing countries of East Asia. According to World Bank data for 1991, only one former communist country, Hungary, had an industrial sector of "average" size. All others were significantly larger. The transition economies in 1991 had, on average, 14 percent more GDP generated in the industrial sector than would be expected, given per capita income (corrected for purchasing power), and 15 percent less GDP generated in services.[13]

Given this imbalance, it was predictable that the transition to a market economy would involve a boom in services and a decline in industry almost everywhere in the FSB.[14] Services were needed. Many were nontradable, protected naturally from international competition. They could be produced economically by small units. They did not require great initial investment in new capital equipment. They ran continuously, not seasonally, so "learning by doing" could proceed at a steady pace. Almost everywhere in the FSB, service activities are booming. The decline of industrial activity was not so pretty. Existing units were huge and vital to their employees. With their useless, energy-hungry capital stocks, they required massive recapitalization. And many operated seasonally, in phase with harvests and weather, entering a crucial cycle only once or twice each year. Such enterprises would find it much more difficult to learn a new technology rapidly.

When a plant in a market economy is unable to sell its output in the market, it cuts back production and may attempt to re-structure and introduce new technology. As production col-lapses, workers lose their jobs. If restructuring fails, managers and supervisors join them. Money dries up, and the firm dies. This sequence of market-driven events has been largely absent when it comes to the huge, inefficient plants of the FSB. Uneco-nomic scale, poor location, and inferior, wasteful equipment mark them out for failure, but this has not been allowed to happen. Relatively rarely have workers been cut loose. Manag-ers—often powerful party functionaries in the old regime—have for the most part survived by using their political skills and connections. Credits have been extended that allow firms to pay workers (though typically less than in the past and often irregularly). Inter-firm debt has mounted as well, deepening the policy dilemma because zombie firms now share the blood sup-ply of potential survivors.[15] And, of course, with supply shrink-ing far faster than demand, with ballooning expansion of credit, inflation has soared.

When external injections of dollars have permitted, people's demand for foreign goods and assets has for a time been satisfied by intervention in foreign exchange markets. Billions of aid dol-lars have been spent to delay the inflationary effects of measures to prop up old, uncompetitive, giant firms, instead of to ease their demise and facilitate the growth of smaller replacements. Ironically, the overvalued exchange rates only add to the competitive burden on producers of tradable goods. The sale of aid dollars mutes the inflationary pressure, but it does not end it. Currency-market intervention has provided classic opportunities for currency speculators, while ordinary citizens simply see inflation and currency depreciation move in bursts rather than steadily. Hundreds of millions of dollars that could have been distributed to citizens through public works programs instead reward those who play foreign exchange markets.

Waiting for the Market

The end of communism offered a remarkable opportunity for visionary leadership to shape the transformation of the FSB, but unfortunately it has gone largely unexploited. No Jean Monnet has emerged from within the transition states with a vision for economic progress. Western advisers, too—represented most pervasively by teams from the IMF and World Bank—have failed to offer imaginative advice. Locked into a rigid model of free-market capitalism, they have been preoccupied with the appearance rather than the substance of structural change.

The painful process of replacing the old communist economy with new firms, new jobs, and new infrastructure is aided only slightly by the standard prescriptions of Western advisers: privatization, liberalization, and macroeconomic austerity. If existing firms cannot survive competition, privatization is of dubious value. Macroeconomic policy must confront the reason for fiscal and monetary undiscipline: the absence of a program to phase out inherited firms. Faced with the choice of abandoning industries and farms to wholesale bankruptcy or providing them with liquidity, governments and central bankers have opted for monetary infusions, that is, inflation.

Rather than accord government a central role in confronting the dilemma of transition, most domestic and international economists appear to have a deist's vision of the role of the public sector: the lawmakers set the "institutional infrastructure" (property and contract law, systems of payment, courts and police), commit themselves to well-defined macroeconomic laws of motion, and then let markets work their magic, unimpeded.

In an inversion of the old socialist dream, both domestic and international economic reformers have set up an idealized vision of the free market against an image of government intervention dominated by deficiency and failure. Thus the Czech leader Vaclav Klaus has called for "a market economy without adjectives," defiantly thumbing his nose at the "social market" states of Northern Europe. Yet in fact, Klaus has supported policies that are far from the laissez-faire ideal. As in every country of the FSB, the Czechs have not permitted failing enterprises to crash noisily to the ground. They have not simply abandoned workers to market forces in housing, health care, and the other services offered by state firms under communism. The Czech Republic, with its long traditions of excellence in manufacturing and sobriety in economic affairs—and its appeal to foreign exchange-rich tourists—has managed the transition better than any other member of the FSB, but not because it abandoned the economic role of the public sector. Why has practice there, as almost everywhere else in the FSB, been so at odds with theory?

If the standard package of the IMF and the World Bank were adopted as prescribed, the results would be brutal. Placed on a hard-budget constraint and ordered to sink or swim as best they could, most firms would sink, and fast. In theory, the people displaced would find work in emerging service enterprises and in new, competitive industrial firms. But in most of the FSB, the economic equivalent of wartime destruction of the capital stock cannot be expected to generate new opportunities smoothly and rapidly enough to absorb the displaced workers. Nor could one assume, as most of the Western advisers implicitly do, that masses of workers raised in a socialist economy could suddenly become independent and entrepreneurial in open labor markets.

In short, democratically elected leaders could not set in motion forces that would cast the population adrift. Their laissez-faire rhetoric notwithstanding, they knew that citizens would not stand idly by while the enterprises around which their lives were organized were reduced to economic rubble. Voters would not stand for it. Yet the rhetoric—and the thinking that lay behind it—deprived the leaders, and their experts, of the ability to devise government economic policies to manage the transition. For the challenge to policy during the transition was not to identify goals that virtually everyone shared—an orderly democratic market economy that is efficient, fair, and macroeconomically stable. It was to establish a new role for government, based on the recognition that government, warts and all, had to be a great part of the solution to problems of the transition.

But ideology made this hard to see. With political winds in the United States and Britain blowing strongly against government, it seemed to many that the central job of restructuring government in the post-Soviet world was simply to disengage government from the economy and get it out of the way. If this reflected the political fashion of the day, it also showed the tendency of late-twentieth-century economics to neglect institutions.

Behind the international agencies' narrow, mechanical policy prescriptions lies a pessimistic view of the potential for productive government intervention and a failure to reckon with the politics of economic policymaking in a democratic society. This approach drives their recommendations away from packages tailored to specific socioeconomic circumstances and toward one-size-fits-all programs based on classical liberalism. The evidence of alternative forms of capitalism—in East Asia, for example—in which government plays an active role, is largely ignored or deemed inappropriate. New Deal policies that were used to mitigate the costs of the Great Depression in the United States are similarly dismissed. Nor is the experience of postwar Western Europe heeded, where Jean Monnet's efforts to coordinate the coal and steel sectors led eventually to the European Community. The narrow economic contribution of any of these government interventions is certainly open to debate. But all of them helped unite and focus societies as they emerged from poverty and economic crisis.

International agencies have not forbidden active government policy to establish a social safety net or to help retire failing industries; but, with few exceptions, neither have they provided leadership in formulating and financing such policies. Market economies everywhere pursue policies that ease the economic pressure on declining sectors and help citizens in distress. Yet international agencies have sought to impose policy that is more "economically correct" than in any Western country.

This is not to suggest that the West bears primary responsibility for the current distress in the FSB, nor to imply that it is within the power of external agencies alone to set matters right. The focus is on opportunities lost, on contributions not made. Indeed, the reluctance of international aid donors to endorse and finance more active programs for government does not mean that people within these institutions have not thought deeply about these issues.

Economist Joshua Aizenman and the IMF's Peter Isard have built a model to justify public subsidies to state-owned firms to slow their demise, thereby preventing the emergence of supply bottlenecks, excessive adjustment costs, and other externalities.[16] Isard and Michael P. Dooley have discussed the need for government intervention, especially in financial markets, in an essay that received the AMEX Bank Review Prize of 1992.[17] In 1991, Eric Rice interviewed forty-two staff members of the World Bank and summarized their ideas about governments' role in the transition. He concludes that "governments of Eastern Europe are obliged to care for the losers in the process of restructuring. . . . Given the region's fiscal constraints and its need for infrastructure, benefit programs that require recipients to work on public infrastructure projects may be of particular interest."[18] Yet when he turns, barely a page later, to "An Agenda for External Assistance," he makes no mention of assistance in establishing and financing such programs.

For it is when the focus shifts from discussion of issues to the actual dispersion of aid that the priorities of the agencies become clear: macroeconomic austerity, privatization, price liberalization, aid for support of exchange rates, plus technical advisers to show how to do all of the above. Aid to the unemployed—say through public employment in large-scale public works programs—is endorsed as a good idea, but only to the extent that governments pursue it on their own through their copious tax revenues.

When it comes to privatization, far more attention has been paid to formalities than to substance. By no means do the formalities ensure that the structure of incentives and rewards faced by workers and, especially, managers will change fundamentally. With centralized control disabled in most of the FSB, most enterprises, privatized or not, are run by managers who respond to complex incentives and constituencies including local politicians, gangsters, workers, and their own personal interests. A ritual of privatization could involve the establishment of an enterprise that truly operates under a hard-budget constraint with its managers accountable to active owners; or it could mean that paper has been shuffled and otherwise nothing has changed for managers or government functionaries. For small enterprises, particularly in the services, an entrepreneurial private sector is growing rapidly. But the "privatization" of manufacturing and farming has brought about much less change than might have been expected.[19]

What Is to Be Done?

To navigate the transition successfully, the governments of the FSB must take responsibility for meeting basic human needs. Citizens will not tolerate the collapse of valued services formerly supplied by enterprises—including housing, health care, and community activities. As part of broader economic restructuring, government needs to disengage such services from firms by offering substitutes. Unfortunately, there is little in the program of international agencies to help them do so; the holy trinity of stabilization, liberalization, and privatization receives almost all prayer and votive offerings, accompanied by stern sermons on the dangers of a bloated public sector.[20] Poland's need to design a pension system that discourages costly early retirement received little international attention until poor policies were introduced. Whether or not one sees health clinics or day care centers as falling within the optimal sphere of government activity, measures to enable the demise of uneconomic enterprises must include support for the people who will suffer.

The specter of corrupt and distorting government intervention must be balanced against the consequences of a lifeless public sector in a sinking economy. What institution but government will provide public goods such as education, public health, and infrastructure? Where can ordinary people turn when, confused and impoverished, they see the world changing around them faster than they can comprehend?

There is an old story of a scientist who knew that he could train a horse to live without food. Weaning the animal day by day, the scientist almost had succeeded when the feckless creature died. The advice was good, the experimental subject was weak. Before the FSB succumbs, the experiment must be revised.

Against the experience of the Czech Republic—which shows that it is possible to move from socialism toward capitalism in a remarkably straight line—we should weigh the inability of the remainder of the FSB to follow suit. While the eventual goal, democratic capitalism, remains unchanged, we must recognize the responsibility of the government not only to put conditions in place that allow competitive markets to develop, but also to play an active role as a midwife to the transition. People will bear the costs of transition only if they have confidence that they have not been abandoned to changes they do not understand.

Three steps are essential. First, none of the responsibility for provision of education, health care, child care, and community activities should rest with firms. Governmental agencies must provide such services. Second, the safety net for the unemployed must be developed, probably based on public works projects. Third, the inevitability of industrial protection must be acknowledged; a structure of protection, its implementation (through subsidies or barriers to international trade), and a timetable for its evolution must be worked out. The problem of transition societies is not simply to remove or reduce intrusive government but to find the proper mix of public and private institutions—to reconstitute government. In the FSB, it is necessary not only to "privatize" socialized firms so that they can sink or swim. It is necessary to "socialize" some functions formerly performed by firms, so that enterprises that cannot make the transition to markets will be able to disappear into bankruptcy without dragging the education, health care, and community-support systems along with them.

Creating a capable and efficient public sector will not be easy. Besides the challenge of establishing a cadre of reliable bureaucrats, reasonably honest and ready to try new methods, there is the problem of financing. Here Western aid can play a central role. Billions of dollars have been spent to support currency values. A half billion dollars could support ten million displaced workers in the FSB for a month. Aid donors would do better to shift support from stabilization to public works and social service programs, as happened in the United States during the New Deal.

Given their history of overwhelming intrusions of government into family and commercial life, it is easy to understand why people throughout the FSB embraced the principle of free markets. Yet the profound inability of post-Soviet industrial and agricultural firms to compete created strong contractionary pressures, the full effects of which have been avoided only because central governments have boosted credits to firms, regardless of whether their long-term prospects are promising or hopeless. International lenders sternly demand that governments abjure monetary excess and force firms to accept the hard consequences of hard budget constraints. The governments promise, and even keep their promises for a time. Workers are not paid; real wages continue to drop; gangsters and hustlers seem to be the only people who prosper. And then the people say no. Reformers are thrown out. Elected governments lose credibility with their constituents, who instead turn to demagogues and economic witch doctors.

Meanwhile, Western advisers stick tenaciously to their prescriptions. Acknowledging only one model of capitalism—the neoclassical economists' paradigm—they fail to adjust the medication to historical and national circumstance. If they had their way, they would push the economies of the FSB further toward the classical liberal paradigm than any Western country.

While some countries of the FSB seem to be managing the transition to capitalism with tolerable success—Estonia and Poland, as well as the Czech Republic—most are not. The sorry spectacle of failed advice, economic decline, and mutual distrust and disrespect between governments and their external advisers suggests no positive outcome. Nor is this likely to change without a general recognition that activist government—one that responds to economic needs and popular distress—has been part of capitalism in almost all times and places. The state cannot simply be the maker and enforcer of economic rules. It will not do for advisers simply to acknowledge a government's right to pursue popular programs if it can find the money to do so. Western advice and resources must foster essential public as well as private institutions; they must build governments' ability to provide public goods; they must strengthen political and economic leadership for the ordinary citizen caught in the maelstrom of transition.

FIVE

· ·

The Chinese Puzzle

Leonard Silk and Mark Silk

We are weeping from too many joys. We are rid of the
shame of the past. Our forefathers can feel at ease in their
graves. O, my Motherland, you are no longer a broken bowl
in front of an ancient temple.

The above lines come from a poem that a man named Qing Xian
sent to the Communist Party newspaper in Guangdong
shortly before the 1989 massacre of pro-democracy demon-
strators in Beijing's Tiananmen Square. The verse neatly encapsu-
lates the model China offers of capitalist economic development;
one that juxtaposes the shame of political repression, symbolized
by the Tiananmen tragedy, with a degree of economic liberalization that has transformed the still officially communist country
into a powerhouse of production and entrepreneurship.

Since 1979, the Chinese economy has grown an average of 9
percent per year—more than double the rate of the previous
twenty years.[1] If China, with its population of over one billion
people, were to continue at this pace, by the third decade of the
twenty-first century its economy would be the world's largest.
Already, China's economic power has been felt globally. Its con-

struction boom, for example, has strained the supply-demand relationship in international steel markets. Its impact on food markets, as a grain importer, is likely to grow rapidly. Driven by a population of over one billion people, the Chinese economy could turn into an engine of growth for the entire world, and the twenty-first century might come to be regarded as "the Chinese Century."

However, there are critics who doubt that the boom of the past two decades can last much longer. They warn that the Chinese economy is overheating, that inefficiency and corruption are widespread, that disparities between rich and poor are growing, and that, having gained so much from importing the available technology of others, China will not be able to keep growing rapidly on its own without more fundamental changes in the system than its communist leaders have thus far been willing to accept. Unless the country achieves political as well as economic freedom, these critics say, a political explosion will drive China back into isolation and stagnation. Nor are the concerns limited to educated Westerners. Chinese peasants still fear a return of traditional Chinese xenophobia. According to the *People's Daily*, many of them are so afraid that the government will change its policy of "making people wealthy" that they are hiding their newly earned cash in their homes or putting it in banks far from their home villages.

Be that as it may, China's economic rise has profound implications for the future of capitalism. The Chinese authoritarian model offers an alternative to other developing countries that could undermine the West's efforts to promote a development model based on democratic values. For however critical free speech and majority rule may seem to be to a successful capitalist system in the long run, authoritarian decisionmaking has enabled China to pursue a controlled, step-by-step approach to a market economy that until now has proved far more successful than the combination of democracy and dismantled economic coordination to be found in Russia and Eastern Europe.

The Takeoff

Today's economic growth in China is the result of a decade and a half of continuous reform. By the late 1970s, the results of the radical economic experiments of the Mao Zedong years had taught the communist leaders that extreme centralization of control and extreme egalitarianism would be disastrous. The "Great Leap Forward" of the late 1950s and the ideological fury of the Cultural Revolution caused sharp falls in agricultural production; over twenty million people died in famines, which were linked to the government's hatred of presumed internal "enemies" and its suppression of truth about conditions on the land. After Mao's death in 1976, radical ideologues were totally discredited; Maoists were eliminated as a serious political force and advocates of Stalinist bureaucracy were crippled. To recoup the "ten lost years" of the Cultural Revolution, the Chinese government turned to Deng Xiaoping to renew the Communist Party's claim to legitimacy by rebuilding the economy. Deng, who returned from his second banishment to become "paramount leader" in 1978, played down ideology, put the class struggle on the back burner, and stressed material incentives to motivate farmers and workers.

The way to economic growth was cracked open by dissolving the old system of collectivized agriculture. Allowing families to farm the land and to decide how, when, and what to produce was the most far-reaching and dramatic of the reforms. To increase incentives for hard work, the government instituted a "production responsibility system," by which tasks were assigned to a family or individuals through contracts between the production team and the household, assuring that the families of farmers would be rewarded for their efforts. By the mid-1980s, almost all farm tasks had been assigned on a household basis. The families, called "brigades" to preserve some flavor of socialist acceptability, were permitted to contract with the government to produce set amounts of particular crops and to sell what they produced above those amounts on local free markets, keeping the cash they earned. They were also encouraged to engage in side-line production and dispose of that as they wished. The government then moved to rely on market forces for distributing farm products, eliminating or sharply reducing quotas for the major crops by 1985. The result: Agricultural output grew two-and-a-half times.

Concurrently, Chinese authorities were making a concerted effort to expand foreign trade. Special economic zones were set up to make it easier for foreign investors and exporters to do business. Centralized state authority over trade was dispersed to regional and provincial corporations, and eventually to domestic industrial enterprises themselves. Foreign exchange was gradually decontrolled. While opening China to foreign trade, Deng encouraged foreign investment as well. New joint-venture regulations were promulgated in 1979, in part because of energy shortages that forced the Chinese government to invite foreign companies to help explore for offshore oil.

By the mid-1980s, the inflow of foreign capital and technologies was exerting an enormous impact on the economy, especially in the coastal areas. Measures were taken to give greater independence to the southeastern province of Guangdong, traditionally active in foreign trade and influenced by Hong Kong. Trading companies were allowed to promote exchange trade with Hong Kong and Macao and to keep their profits. A State Statistical Bureau communique issued on March 18, 1992, reported that at the end of 1991, 37,215 foreign-funded enterprises were producing $12 billion worth of exports, representing 17 percent of the export total.

During the first four years of reform, direct foreign investment grew by less than $2 billion. By 1991, however, the contracted capital inflow doubled, and in 1992, it had more than quadrupled, as foreign investors signed agreements for $57.5 billion in future investment and actually poured into China $11.2 billion. In 1993, foreign investment contracts reached an amazing $100 billion, and foreign direct investment that year rose to about $20 billion. Much of this influx came from investments in joint ventures and emerging financial markets by overseas Chinese in Hong Kong, Taiwan, Singapore, Indonesia, and the United States. Yet it is important to note that, with a domestic savings rate typical of East Asia—30 percent—China was generating most of its capital internally. Altogether, exports surged from $14.8 billion in 1979 to $85 billion in 1992. Now ranking tenth in world trade, China has already become an important trading partner to many countries, including the United States.

Last in line was reform of the Chinese industrial sector, which did not begin in earnest until 1984 with the abolition of regional monopolies and the establishment of a dual-price system that permitted inputs and outputs to be sold at prices set by the market as well as by the state. This had the effect of encouraging villages and townships to develop competitive businesses of their own. The growth of locally based enterprise, especially light manufacturing and retail businesses, served the government's aim of promoting a shift from producer to consumer goods, the production of which required less energy in the wake of the oil crisis of the late 1970s. It also enabled tens of millions of surplus farm workers to switch to industrial jobs, so that by the early 1990s, over one-fifth of China's rural population was working in light industries.

Another component of China's industrial policy involved reducing military budgets and manpower. In 1985, the People's Liberation Army's eleven military regions were cut to seven and the number of senior officers halved. The Central Intelligence Agency estimates that from 1984 to 1988 China's military spending fell 21 percent.[2] Meanwhile, the armed forces helped manage the shift from military to civilian production. The Chinese government claims that production of civilian goods and services now accounts for 65 percent of defense-sector economic activity, including construction, health services, transport, telecommunications, farming, and even entertainment centers and massage parlors. These enterprises, according to the *Wall Street Journal*, now generate most of the $6 billion needed annually to pay for the three-million-member armed forces.[3]

It is important to recognize that industrial reform has not meant privatization. The vast majority of township and village enterprises are collectives owned by local government. China's leaders judged it both inconsistent with socialist ideology and unwise public policy to privatize the large, state-owned industrial enterprises. For although these often antiquated and inefficient enterprises represent a large drain on the national budget, they employ huge numbers of workers and provide them with housing, health care, and other services. In fact, half of all Chinese city-dwellers are housed by state enterprises. The government's decision to prop up these enterprises by keeping energy prices artificially low has also contributed to the financial burden; in the early 1990s, fully 40 percent of state-enterprise losses came from the coal mining and petroleum extraction industries. Some efforts have been made to reduce the number of state-enterprise workers and to place some in more competitive, spin-off businesses. But selling the enterprises to private investors or simply shutting them down has been deemed too high a price to pay in terms of social dislocation.

After over a decade of industrial reform, only 10 percent of Chinese industry could be considered private in an economy in which industry accounted for 50 percent of output and 80 percent of total exports. From this, economists Gary Jefferson and Thomas Rawski concluded: "China's experience of industrial reform suggests that economists tend to overstate the importance of early privatization during the transition process. The strength of government efforts to force enterprises toward financial independence may count for more than the locus of ownership."[4] The evidence for this, at least so far, would appear to be indisputable.

According to the Chinese government, the gross national product nearly quadrupled from $120 billion in 1980 to $427 billion in 1989. After a brief setback caused by anti-inflationary measures in 1988–89, China's economy again grew very rapidly—in real terms, by 7 percent in 1991, 12.8 percent in 1992, and 14 percent in 1993. But if anything, government figures understate the extent of the growth. Whereas, for example, the official estimate of GNP per capita for 1991 was $370, the International Monetary Fund re-estimated it at $1,450 by pricing all Chinese goods according to estimated purchasing power. An Australian study, based on food consumption patterns, concludes that a proper estimate of China's GNP would be double or triple that of the official statistics. The discrepancy between official statistics and independent estimates derives mainly from the artificially suppressed prices in the socialist system and the disparity in the valuation of a variety of products. This may reflect policy: By appearing to be poorer on paper than they are in reality, the Chinese can enjoy benefits in borrowing and trade that apply only to the poorest countries. In any event, the discrepancy should begin to disappear as prices continue to be liberalized from a condition of almost complete control when Deng came to power. Since the agricultural reforms of 1978, about three-quarters of state-fixed farm prices have been abolished, while by 1992 the government controlled prices of only 44 percent of industrial product sales. China's burgeoning capital markets are striking evidence of its shift toward a market economy.

Question Marks

Although it has kept economic dislocations to a minimum, China's staged approach to development has created numerous opportunities for corruption. Enterprise heads have been able to profiteer by exploiting the differences between state-set and market prices. Bureaucrats-turned-businessmen defy edicts from Beijing in order to pursue short-term gains. Nepotism and favoritism within business and industry are widespread.

One notorious scandal took place on Hainan Island, a designated "open area" where local officials engaged in a scheme to enrich themselves through sales of expensive cars and other consumer goods, instead of using scarce foreign exchange for purchases of capital equipment. Nor was Hainan an isolated case. In its wake, the government announced it was investigating

200,000 cases of "unscrupulous profiteering, tax evasion and violation of business regulations." Deng told the nation: "Only socialism can eliminate the greediness, corruption and injustice which are inherent in capitalism. . . . In recent years, production has gone up, but the pernicious influence of capitalism and feudalism has not been reduced to a minimum. Instead, evils that had long been extinct after liberation have come to life again."

To be sure, neither Deng nor other high officials showed any signs of reversing course as they tried to achieve a more open economy. In Beijing and in the special economic zones of Shenzhen and Xiamen, officials took a common line, at once promising that they would do everything to eradicate corruption and denouncing party opponents who sought to use its existence as an argument for trying to stop economic reforms and the open-door policy. Urging foreign corporations to invest in their country, the officials insisted that there would never be a change in their openness to foreign investment and the safeguarding of foreign property and rights to repatriate capital and earnings.

In private interviews, American and other foreign businessmen in Shanghai have complained that serious problems do exist for foreign investors, mainly involving the readiness of the Chinese government to break a contract it doesn't like. The Chinese have been sensitive to the criticism, saying that "issues not covered by present laws and regulations may be incorporated into economic contracts stipulating in explicit terms the rights and obligations of both parties." According to them, the contracts, once approved by the government, "have full legal effect." But, say the foreign businessmen, bureaucratic snarls or other tie-ups sometimes prevent government approval of what they thought was a valid contract. They call for a stricter enforcement of Chinese laws protecting foreign investors, as well as improvement of the laws themselves.

If China's socialist legal system has lacked protections for foreign investors, it has likewise been inadequate to protect the natural environment from the consequences of rapid industrialization. Air pollution in Beijing is four to six times as bad as it was in Tokyo at its worst levels in the late 1960s. Overall damage to China's land, air, water, and forests—including related health care costs—has been calculated at 15 percent of GNP. Researchers at the Chinese Academy of Sciences predict that if measures are not taken to protect the environment, China will face severe environmental crises in the first two decades of the twenty-first century.[5]

At the same time, rapid industrialization has created a workplace environment reminiscent of the worst of the Western industrial sweatshops of the late nineteenth and early twentieth centuries. According to Uli Schmetzer of the *Chicago Tribune,* 19,000 Chinese workers died in industrial accidents in the first half of 1993; in Guangdong province alone, a factory fire occurred every day. Factory owners habitually ignore safety regulations, compensating workers with pittances for loss of life and limb.[6] Strikes against these sweatshop conditions by workers in foreign factories in Guangdong and Fujian have led investors to seek more compliant workers in interior provinces, a process that facilitated the government's desire to have prosperity spread from the southeast coast into the hinterland. Despite success in creating jobs for displaced agricultural workers, an army of 50 million now travel around the country in search of any available work, and their numbers are expected to double or triple in the coming years.

While in the West advocates of laissez faire minimize and

even dismiss the need for macroeconomic management, observers of the Chinese scene worry about the degree to which decentralization has undermined Beijing's ability to keep the country's economic house in order with fiscal and monetary policy. In place of a uniform national system of taxation, the provinces negotiate their own deals with Beijing, and then proceed to find ways to minimize what they contribute. As a result, central-government tax receipts shrunk in half relative to gross domestic product between 1980 and 1991, and it has become exceedingly difficult to coordinate taxing and spending policy, whether to manage the economy or to make infrastructure improvements. On the monetary side, weak central banking authority has made it increasingly difficult for Beijing to keep inflation under control. In late 1993, for example, urban consumer prices rose 20 percent in an economy overheated by double-digit growth rates and speculation in real property, foreign exchange, and stocks. The head of the central bank was fired and replaced with Deputy Prime Minister Zhu Rongji, who announced a set of anti-inflation policies. But with provinces able to issue bonds to finance enterprise (in addition to abundant foreign and domestic private capital), reining in inflation proved more difficult than previously. If inflation is permitted to stop the flow of domestic savings that has fueled China's boom, the costs—political as well as economic—could be huge.

Human Rights

In a petition to the Chinese government released the day before the arrival of U.S. Secretary of State Warren Christopher in Beijing on his ill-fated trip of March, 1994, seven senior Chinese

intellectuals issued a statement citing these words from the
United Nations Declaration of Human Rights:

- Nobody shall carry out unreasonable arrests, detentions,
  and deportations.
- Everybody has the right to freedom of ideas, conscience,
  and religion.
- Everybody has the right to enjoy the freedom of advocacy
  and expression of views.

Those rights may be crucial to a people's happiness and self-
respect, but how much do they contribute to economic well-
being? China's communist leaders have never promised democratic political reform, and it can be argued that their retention
of an authoritarian political structure has helped them to manage
the difficult transition to a market economy more successfully
than Russia and the Eastern European countries. Certainly it has
earned them some awed respect from economists, international
civil servants, government officials, and above all from business
people, whose ability to make money might actually be inhibited
under a democratic system that, for example, passed minimum
wage or workplace safety laws.

Is the Chinese model of authoritarian capitalism one that other
developing countries can or should imitate? China is by no
means the only country in East Asia to make rapid economic
progress. Japan achieved an annual growth rate of nearly 10
percent in the 1960s, and South Korea, Taiwan, Singapore, and
Hong Kong followed suit in the 1970s and 1980s. All of these
Asian nations share a common Confucian cultural heritage. (In
response to the question, "What do all the developing countries
that have succeeded in achieving economic take-offs have in
common?" John Kenneth Galbraith jokingly asserted: "They are

all Chinese.") Yet each of the others followed a different pattern of development than China's.

Their political environments have ranged along a spectrum from rigid autocracy to open democracy. Japan's postwar economic expansion occurred within a democratic political system, as did Hong Kong's. South Korea and Taiwan started their economic development under authoritarian military regimes, but both have recently democratized their political systems. For its part, Singapore has become more rigid and authoritarian over the years.

The question remains how long China's apparent success with its repressive model can endure. As the examples of Nazi Germany, fascist Italy, and the Soviet bloc have shown, totalitarianism has its limits. Whether the Chinese leaders like it or not, their economic reforms have empowered the Chinese people to a far greater extent than in the Mao years. Economic progress has given them greater self-respect and hope of improving their lives; economic freedom has made them more self-reliant. It is in the nature of a market economy to put a premium on individual choice and initiative, to instill yearnings for freedom and protection from state intrusion. Tiananmen may have squashed the public democracy movement, but it is hard to believe that, over time, popular demands for political freedom will not grow. Ultimately, there is a chance that China could follow the South Korea/Taiwan model, with economic development eventually bringing about political liberalization.

Meanwhile, Deng's open-door policy, by fostering interdependence with foreign countries, has made China vulnerable to outside pressure. Western suspension of loan and aid programs in the wake of the Tiananmen massacre forced China to cut back imports to preserve its foreign exchange reserves. Zhu Rongji, the deputy premier, was told on a visit to Tokyo that Japanese foreign aid to China would depend on the level of its military spending—a warning for restraint that China has not ignored. And the U.S. threat to cancel China's Most Favored Nation (MFN) status because of its human rights abuses would have cost Beijing billions of dollars and hundreds of thousands of jobs.

To be sure, President Clinton's decision to drop the threat, in response to American business pressures, brought not just a sense of relief but a renewed arrogance from Beijing. Soon after U.S. renewal of its MFN privileges, the Chinese decided to explode a hydrogen bomb, as if marking a triumph with a display of fireworks. This kind of nose-thumbing, designed to demonstrate that all such threats are paper tigers, is predicated on a belief that transnational business interests will never permit Western governments to deny them access to the biggest emerging market in the world.

For the United States, China's human rights record is only the most visible source of tension between the two countries. There are also the issues of China's large trade surplus; its military power, which some see as a threat to stability in the Asian Pacific region; and its arms sales, which strengthen aggressive and dictatorial states in other parts of the world. Along these lines, some geopolitical strategists argue that a more pragmatic and "nuanced" relationship would better serve the interests of both the United States and China, and avoid a confrontation that could inflict heavy damage on world economic development.

A Policy Impact Panel established by the Council on Foreign Relations and chaired by former Secretaries of State Henry Kissinger and Cyrus Vance, concluded: "China has its issues and we have ours. Each of us should promote our positions to suit our interests, while recognizing that we have a common overriding interest in making things work out without backing away from our values. We should therefore remain in constant strategic dialogue with Beijing so as to avoid a situation in which policy failures in any one sphere—whether in human rights, nonproliferation, trade, Asian regional issues, or other matters—undermine Sino-U.S. cooperation across the board."[7] President Clinton apparently accepted this logic and backed away from his earlier efforts to link human rights reforms to U.S. trade with China.

On this matter, Iraq may offer a cautionary example. Throughout the 1980s, Iraq's President Saddam Hussein and his diplomats emphasized their country's stability and growth in an attempt to mute criticism of their egregious human rights violations. Baghdad enjoyed considerable respect from Western nations, including the United States, which provided it with military and economic assistance. But as Iraq's invasion of Kuwait showed, rewarding dictators and tacitly encouraging their aggressive designs can be a dangerous and costly game. During the past two decades, Chinese leaders have subordinated geopolitical ambitions to economic development, but there is no guarantee that they will continue to do so. Historically, China has shown a tendency to bully its neighbors, and should its growing economic power turn into greater political assertiveness, it would create serious problems for countries throughout the Pacific area—including the United States. The Beijing government has already stepped up efforts to modernize the military and has increased both its arms procurement from, and its own arms sales to, other countries. It has also rattled its saber at the island state of Taiwan, to which it has never surrendered territorial claim.

Yet Chinese leaders know they don't hold all the cards. Hong

Kong, which officially becomes part of China in 1997, has invested close to 70 percent of China's total intake of foreign capital, and Beijing must be wary of brutal behavior that would provoke the Hong Kongese into pulling their capital (and themselves) out—or at least suspending further investment on the mainland. Beijing must also worry about destroying its growing trade and investment relations with Taiwan. Nor can all the economic success in the world erase its unpleasant image as a trampler of human rights. In 1995, its repression of dissidents was once again dramatized by the arrest, trial, and expulsion of human rights activist Harry Wu. Likewise, the regime's heavy-handed behavior in hosting the United Nations Fourth World Conference on Women proved to be an international embarrassment.

Are the Chinese leaders ready to loosen their grip over the people? They know that the greatest challenge to their dominance will ultimately come from within—from students and workers, from scientists and business people, from intellectuals and farmers, whose power can only grow as the economy advances. They fear that granting political rights would undermine their monopoly of power—power that has enabled them to line their own pockets and those of their friends. The Tiananmen massacre in effect compelled Chinese leaders to make the promotion of wealth the sole basis of its legitimacy, and indeed, there is some evidence that this approach has worked—that the populace, alienated from all politics, has focused its attention largely on the achievement of material prosperity.[8] China may well decide that the price of being a human-rights pariah is worth paying, at least for the foreseeable future. Its success in this regard encourages other developing countries to follow the dictum: "If your economy is growing, you can repress your people."

SIX

....

Japan at the Crossroads

Leonard Silk and Mark Silk

The persistence of Japan's huge trade surplus, based on Tokyo's determination to acquire external assets rather than invest domestically, has raised the question of whether Japanese capitalism is essentially incompatible with capitalism in the West. Indeed, some economists maintain that if the Japanese system is permitted to continue, it will undermine the world economic system. Supporting aggressive efforts to force Japan to open its markets and the use of managed trade as a means of getting a "fair share" of those markets, a number of ranking Clinton trade and economic officials did not hesitate to admit sharing these "revisionist" views. As Laura d'Andrea Tyson, the former chairman of the President's Council of Economic Advisers, put it, "Japan's capitalism differs from America's, so that sometimes quotas are the only possible solution."[1]

The premise of the revisionist argument is that "traditional"

Japanese society has created a political and economic system that exploits the openness of the West. Not sharing the Judeo-Christian heritage, the Japanese are, it is charged, individually and collectively hostile to outsiders and to Western conceptions of openness. Thus, while Japan has adopted the forms of Western capitalism and democracy, its political-economic system is implacably and unalterably opposed to both.

This point of view gained strength after the end of the Cold War shifted the focus of American foreign policy from containing communism to pursuing economic interests. According to Chalmers Johnson, a leading revisionist, the need to maintain a united anti-communist front led the West in general, and American administrations in particular, to ignore the distinctive, and disruptive, nature of Japanese capitalism. But now, postwar capitalist unity has begun to crack.[2] Hence the Clinton administration's attempts to devise an industrial policy and a tougher trade policy against Japan.

Recent reformist efforts to bring the Japanese economy more into line with the open-market principles of the rest of the industrialized world have failed to change the revisionist image of "Japan, Inc." as a conspiratorial, state-led economic monolith.[3] How warranted is it?

Japanese Social Values

Japanese capitalism has unquestionably been shaped by traditional Japanese culture. Although many Japanese are themselves unconscious of its influence, Confucianism still animates their attachment to authority, seniority, hierarchy, harmony, and continuity, while at the same time denigrating individualism, confrontation, and sudden change. These values, particularly anti-individualism, have given a distinctly nonwestern cast to both the political and the economic system in Japan. Nonconformity, American-style, is anathema to most Japanese, who take comfort not from individual self-expression but from having a clearly defined place within a social hierarchy. Indeed, the Japanese seem to have changed little since Ruth Benedict described their reverence for hierarchy in *The Chrysanthemum and the Sword* fifty years ago.

Japanese economic life is meticulously structured. Hierarchy exists not only within a given company but also within an industry, which is itself part of a larger hierarchy extending, at least nominally, on up through the central government to the emperor. People are expected to obey directives from those above; popular sovereignty, the foundation of Western democracy, goes against the grain. Altogether, Japanese citizens are far readier than Westerners to acquiesce in anti-democratic practices and the abuse of political power. In a society where individualism is seen as egotism, people seek the comfort of groups, the security of organizations. Westerners are often frustrated by Japanese reluctance to accept personal responsibility or even to clarify where it lies; they come away with an impression of Japan as a fortified camp.

In addition, Japan's geographic and historic isolation, and its high degree of ethnic homogeneity, have fostered a strong national identity as well as an obsession with "Japaneseness." Despite a high degree of interaction with foreigners in recent years, the Japanese maintain the ideal of a closed society, discriminating against foreigners on the grounds that they are not "Japanese." (Such foreigners include ethnic Koreans and Chinese who speak Japanese as their native language and whose families have lived in Japan for generations.) In economic life, the Japanese have kept foreign businessmen at bay for over a century with nontariff barriers.

Japanese cultural values and social structure are nowhere better expressed than in education. Japanese parents pull out all the stops to qualify their children for the best nursery schools, which are seen as a necessary first step to the best jobs. Cram courses designed to generate the highest test scores begin in elementary school. The highest scorers on college entrance examinations get into the handful of elite universities, which determine future careers and social status, and supply the next generation of leaders of the Japanese establishment.

Postwar Legacies

As important as the Confucian legacy remains in Japanese society today, however, Japanese capitalism has been crucially shaped by the terms of the country's reconstruction after World War II. Initially denied sovereignty and kept from participating in international politics, the Japanese were later prohibited by their constitution from almost any military activity beyond self-defense. The post-occupation security arrangements, under which Japan relied for its national security on U.S. protection, left economic development as virtually the sole outlet for Japanese national ambition. Desperate to reconstruct their devastated country and eager to forget their dark militarist past, the Japanese seized the opportunity with unprecedented fervor.

In the first period of reconstruction, American occupation officials—many of whom were optimistic and committed New Dealers—put through democratic reforms of the Japanese economic structure. They eliminated the "zaibatsu" cartels, instituted anti-monopoly and labor laws, and put in place a fair trade commission. But with the onset of the Cold War, and especially after the Chinese communists came to power in 1949 and war broke out on the Korean Peninsula in 1950, liberal reform gave way to the imperative of transforming Japan as quickly as possible into a politically stable and economically powerful nation that would be impervious to communist subversion. Decentralization and democratization policies were set aside; purged wartime governmental officials were reinstated; antitrust policy was weakened; and new restrictions were imposed on labor unions.

During the 1950s, the Truman and Eisenhower administrations helped build up Japan with Korean War military contracts, hundreds of millions of dollars in aid, and construction loans arranged through the World Bank. The U.S. government also sought to "manage" Japanese trade by encouraging an aggressive export drive while at the same time fostering domestic protectionist practices that enabled Japan's market to become the most closed in the industrialized world. Thirty years later, these policies would come back to haunt Washington.

In Japan, the quest for economic regeneration became a kind of religious crusade. Wartime sacrifices for the emperor were replaced by sacrifices for economic development. Like the kamikaze pilots who believed their sacred spirits could lead imperial Japan to victory, high governmental officials and lowly factory workers alike came to feel that only their dedication and self-sacrifice could save and rebuild the war-battered nation. Poverty-stricken, the Japanese nonetheless restrained their consumption; they enthusiastically embraced the government's "Buy Japanese" campaign. While living standards, leisure, and social capital investment were largely neglected, industrialization and export growth became the shrines at which all worshiped. Tokyo instituted policies to protect and develop infant industries through subsidies, tax breaks, and import restrictions. It also encouraged private savings and facilitated capital investment in strategic industries.

Thus did wartime defeat breed a widespread psychological attitude of self-sacrifice and a "must-do" spirit. But economic success also reinforced traditional Japanese feelings of cultural superiority and isolation, and heightened economic nationalism. It shifted public attention farther and farther away from domestic politics and foreign policy. In creating the world's most remarkable economic success story, it also created the world's most entrenched and nationalistic economy.

The Iron Triangle

Japan's desperate postwar condition caused the government to play a prominent role in the economy, and that role continued once the country was back on its feet. In the 1950s, the government allocated foreign exchange and instituted tax policies intended to increase capital formation. In the 1960s and 1970s, it targeted strategic industries—those deemed to be vital to modern economic development—and vigorously promoted exports. Such aggressively pro-business measures were adopted on the assumption that the Japanese economy was still weak and vulnerable, an assumption that influences Japanese policymakers to this day. Protection of domestic industries has become accepted as a natural way of life.

Through the postwar decades, elite government bureaucrats built relationships with elected politicians and businessmen, creating what has come to be known as the "Iron Triangle" of the Japanese Establishment. Cozy, clubby, and lucrative, the Iron Triangle has safeguarded the interests of its members, while excluding outsiders and newcomers. The key to this tripartite fortress has been the bureaucracy, which has jealously guarded its power and prerogatives through an enormous variety of regulatory devices.

During more than four decades of government-led economic development, the bureaucrats established elaborate industry-protection mechanisms. Various ministries found their reason for being in the protection of industries under their jurisdiction, justifying a wide range of regulatory practices and large staffs to administer them. Japanese capitalism entails extensive supervision and close monitoring by governmental authority, for only within parameters set by the relevant bureaucrats have Japanese businesses been able to compete for profit.

The bureaucrats have guaranteed their power through extensive connections built up while serving in a variety of powerful government positions. Upon their retirement, most senior officials in government ministries are offered executive positions at large companies in a practice known as "amakudari," or "descent from heaven." Each side benefits, as the "descendants" function both as liaisons to their former ministries and effective representatives of them. The bureaucrats also develop special relationships with elected politicians, often by way of former associates in their ranks; one out of five members of the long-dominant Liberal Democratic Party is a former bureaucrat.

The bureaucrats' power is not limitless. Most senior ministry officials are appointed only with the approval or acquiescence of politicians. And in highly politicized issues such as governmental reform or Japan's military role in the world, it is the politicians who decide. But otherwise, the bureaucrats run the country. Senior Japanese politicians usually give carte blanche to top ministry officials, making them the de facto policy-makers as well as the implementers of policy. Lacking vital skills and staff to deal with day-to-day administrative issues, the politicians reserve only the right to grant the technocrats' decisions their final approval, and this is often no more than a rubber stamp. In the meantime, they devote most of their time to party politics and factional strife.

Four decades of one-party rule has had much to do with the decay of the political process. Formed in 1955, the Liberal Democratic Party (LDP) built its appeal through strong anti-communism and a close alliance with the United States—in contrast to the Communist and Socialist Parties, which opposed the U.S.-Japan mutual security agreement. Concerned that a leftist government might come to power, Washington not only underwrote Japan's economic development but provided covert assistance to the LDP. By the 1970s, thanks largely to Prime Minister Hayato Ikeda's campaign to double personal income, the LDP had monopolized the credit for the postwar economic miracle. Meanwhile, the U.S. return of Okinawa, withdrawal from Vietnam, and establishment of relations with China persuaded the Japanese people to accept Washington's military umbrella without question.

Consolidating their power, LDP politicians became crucial intermediaries between big business and the bureaucrats. The politicians assumed special "portfolios"—regulatory authority over particular economic sectors such as agriculture, construction, transportation, and communication; known as that sector's "zoku" or tribe, these politicians were given contributions in order to back favorable legislation and block undesirable government actions. At the local level, politicians received votes and ample political donations from the business establishment through support groups known as "koenkai." Once elected, the politicians returned the favors with regulatory approval and public work contracts.

Money politics also served political ambitions within the LDP. In the late 1960s, Prime Minister Kakuei Tanaka used substantial contributions from the construction industry to expand the power of his own political faction. Soon other factions were scrambling to do the same. Eventually Tanaka was forced to resign and convicted of taking a $2.1 million bribe from the Lockheed Corporation. But though comparable to Watergate in scale, the affair barely affected the course of Japanese politics. Scandal followed scandal during the 1980s, accelerating as the bubble economy expanded the quantity of easy money available to contributors. The Recruit Cosmos scandal forced Prime Minister Noboru Takeshita out of power and tarnished the reputations of former Prime Minister Yasuhiro Nakasone and Finance Minister Kiichi Miyazawa. The Sagawa Kyubin scandal revealed a close connection between LDP leaders and organized crime groups known as "yakuza"; after a public outcry, the leader of one LDP faction resigned from the Diet and was indicted on tax evasion charges. In 1993, having become a national embarrassment, the LDP finally lost an election.

The Entrenched Economy

Japan's postwar obsession with prosperity and growth led government and business to work hand in hand to meet centrally planned goals. The focus was industrial development; consumers were promised that, in the long run, they would benefit through job creation and an abundance of mass-produced and affordable goods. The government's promotion of large business enterprises accorded nicely with the Japanese love of hierarchy, and brought about harmony and stability in economic life. It also proved to be an enormously successful competitive strategy, as large Japanese companies grew faster than their foreign competitors and rapidly expanded their shares of overseas markets. To be sure, behind the success of many Japanese big businesses were countless sacrifices made by the smaller business partners, suppliers, and distributors who relied upon them for their survival.

Contradicting classical Western economic theory, Japanese economic policy has given pride of place to producers rather than consumers. After forty years of rapid economic development, Japanese consumers continue to pay much higher prices than consumers in the West for the same goods and services, and Japanese producers earn larger profit margins than their foreign competitors. Unlike Western countries, no strong consumer-advocate movement has taken root in Japan. High Japanese retail prices result from the exclusion of foreign goods, from monopoly and price-fixing by big business, and from disguised unemployment, ineffective distribution systems, and collusive supplier-buyer relationships.

The Japanese economy is a trust-buster's nightmare. Even before U.S. postwar occupation ended, the old zaibatsu cartels had been permitted to regroup under the name of "keiretsu." With sovereignty restored, the Japanese government lifted the ban on cross-shareholding and interlocking boards of directors, permitting most major Japanese firms to form networks of companies surrounding banks and trading corporations. Like the zaibatsu, the new keiretsu groups acquired companies in almost all major sectors of the Japanese economy, helping one another across industries by sharing information, financial facilities, distribution networks, and trading firms. The lack of enforcement of antitrust laws permitted vertical integration; large firms developed captive distribution networks and maintained exclusive suppliers.

In theory, Japanese market mechanisms are no different from those of other industrialized market economies. In practice, they often do not guarantee free competition to their participants. This is due not only to the keiretsu, but also to the Japanese tradition of maintaining longstanding business relationships even when better goods and services can be procured elsewhere. In addition, the Japanese regulatory system protects small- and medium-sized business by maintaining a complex and inefficient distribution system, and imposes complicated rules on dealers and retailers in end-consumer markets. Recent revelations of widespread bid-rigging practices in the construction industry are but another sign of the lack of free competition in Japanese markets.

As a resource-poor country, Japan had long promoted exports in order to obtain raw materials, but in the postwar era expansion through exports became the primary driving force for Japan's economic growth. The Japanese government targeted strategic industries and protected them from foreign competition until they became sufficiently competitive. It also prevented the entry of foreign companies into Japan by restricting their activities through licensing and joint ventures. The result was to create chronic overcapacity within Japan, pushing companies to seek bigger markets at all costs. Often, the government permitted Japanese firms to fix high domestic prices even as they dumped their products abroad at prices far below the cost of production.

Driven by overcapacity, the intense export drive produced a chronic trade imbalance—and complaints by foreign competitors that when it came to Japan, trade was not a two-way street.

Here there is no underestimating the role of mammoth general trading firms called "Sogo Shosha," which until very recently served as the principal intermediaries between Japan and the outside world. For in addition to procuring raw materials and finding overseas markets, the Sogo Shosha functioned as shields against undesirable foreign competitors, selecting imports for Japanese markets in such a way as to protect their affiliated manufacturers.

The trade balance was also exacerbated by the "lifetime employment system" that spread through the Japanese economy after World War II. Geared to rapid growth, businesses devised the system in order to assure a sufficient labor force and keep their skilled workers. It also helped establish and maintain company loyalty. While obligated to take care of employees' well-being, management could count on employees to stay with their company until they retired, and that in turn permitted a much larger investment in employee training and education than would otherwise have been justifiable. Bringing social stability and welfare to Japanese society, the lifetime employment system at the same time created substantial rigidities in the Japanese labor market. And in hard times it invariably led managers at large firms to expand their overseas markets rather than break the taboo against layoffs by reducing capacity.

Unraveling Japan, Inc.

But however much postwar Japanese capitalism differed from the industrialized countries of the West, it was not something unknown under the Western sun. It represented, rather, a throwback to the mercantilism that mainstream Western economics had set itself against since the days of Adam Smith. Indeed, all the elements of Japan's economic system—the push for exports and limits on imports, the internal and external nontariff barriers to free trade, the cartels and monopolistic trading companies— can be seen detailed in the hundreds of pages of *Wealth of Nations* that Smith devoted to attacking mercantilism in early-modern Europe. Moreover, Western economic practice had itself been a far cry from the free-trade orthodoxy of Smith and his intellectual progeny. The United States maintained high tariff barriers throughout the nineteenth century, and remained enamored of at least certain kinds of trade protectionism until World War II. The very fact that Washington was, for reasons of state, eager to sponsor a protectionist Japan in the early days of the Cold War shows the continued appeal of mercantilist policies in jumpstarting an underdeveloped or supine economy.

It can hardly be doubted that mercantilism—undergirded by the willingness of the Japanese people to sacrifice for the greater good of the nation—worked very well for the Japanese up to a point. The question is whether, as a fully mature capitalist economy, Japan can stay its course in the face of foreign pressures to liberalize, growing internationalism within the Japanese business community, and resistance from the Japanese public itself. For in spite of everything, Japanese society has not been unaffected by engagement in the global economy and by the very wealth this engagement has brought. Especially among the young, a new individualism has begun to take hold. Increasing numbers of Japanese now resist self-sacrifice for either the state or the company, preferring instead the pleasures of consumption. The Strategic Impediments Initiative talks between Japan and the United States, aimed at cracking open the Japanese market, helped educate Japanese consumers to their own stake in freer markets, as American negotiators shifted their emphasis from "fairness" for

U.S. producers to consumer benefits for the Japanese. During the 1993 economic summit in Tokyo, President Clinton stressed the theme of consumer benefits when he addressed Japanese students at Waseda University.

Japanese political leaders have increasingly found it in their interest to identify with consumers, particularly in urban areas. Before his downfall in 1993, Prime Minister Kiichi Miyazawa, an old LDP warhorse, proposed somewhat comically that Japan become a "life-style superpower." Elite civil servants themselves are changing. The government as a whole, led by the Labor Ministry, spearheaded a crusade to cut work hours; now government offices are closed Saturdays and workaholic elite bureaucrats can be found taking extended vacations. Even the Ministry of International Trade and Industry (MITI), long regarded as the heart of "Japan, Inc.," has decided to espouse "humane policies" designed to enhance the quality of life by promoting leisure time and the creation of "social capital."

Japanese businessmen are aware of the need to appease rising consumer discontent. Despite having benefitted from the existing system, they increasingly emphasize the need to open the country to foreign competition in order to reduce the trade surplus. At a meeting with American businessmen in Cleveland in 1993, Gaishi Hiraiwa, former chairman of the Japanese Federation of Economic Organizations (the country's most influential business organization), said that a national consensus was emerging in Japan on the need to move from a producer-oriented society to one oriented more to consumers and focused less on exporting.[4] This newfound consumerism on the part of big business has not a little to do with the fact that Japan's internationally competitive enterprises, no longer in need of governmental protection, would prefer some deregulation. In addition, by erasing fears of a socialist threat to Japanese capitalism, the end of the Cold War has removed an important rationale for funneling money to the LDP. Business leaders openly argue that companies and business service organizations should discontinue their financial contributions to political parties.

The increased power and sense of security of the Japanese business community has tended to make companies more resistant to government direction and control. Thus, while MITI officials still map out industrial targets, large firms look the other way and follow their own agendas. The inability of the Ministry of Finance to devise effective fiscal and monetary policies has deepened the disenchantment of Japanese business leaders with bureaucratic guidance. And as the bureaucrats lose control of Japanese business, the rigidities in the postwar Japanese economy are beginning to ease.[5]

Uncertainties and Recession

The defeat of the LDP in July, 1993, seemed to signal not only the end of the Cold War regime of anti-communism and economic growth at all costs but also a fracturing of the Iron Triangle. During the following eight months, the reformist Hosokawa government delivered what LDP leaders had long avoided: electoral reform, the opening of the rice markets, various deregulatory measures, and a more straightforward apology for Japan's transgressions in World War II. However, Hosokawa stepped down in the face of alleged financial irregularities in the spring of 1994 and the successor coalition government came to an end after only two months when the Socialists bolted from the coalition and formed a once unthinkable political alliance with the

LDP. The two former rivals successfully snatched power from the reformists and shoved their agenda onto the back burner.

Nevertheless, the old status quo proved irretrievable. A weakened Iron Triangle left the LDP incapable of implementing effective national policies. Bureaucrats became even freer than before to pursue narrow agendas. And big businesses were left on their own to cope with the strong yen and the protracted recession.

Without strong leadership, little progress was made in trade negotiations with the Americans. In response to President Clinton's call for a "result-oriented" trade policy, the Japanese side continued to argue that setting numerical targets would lead to managed trade and adamantly resisted the use of quotas or benchmarks to measure progress in opening markets to disputed goods. Frustrated by the lack of progress, the Clinton administration announced in May, 1995, that it would impose a 100 percent tariff on thirteen Japanese-made luxury cars. This unilateral threat, which drew criticism both inside and outside the United States, was withdrawn at the end of June after intense negotiations resulted in a compromise. Although the U.S. trade representative, Mickey Kantor, and the Japanese Minister for International Trade and Industry, Ryutaro Hashimoto (soon to be the next Prime Minister), publicly disagreed over whether the compromise contained numerical targets, Clinton's economic officials concluded that the aggressive strategy had worked and began issuing new threats in negotiations on air cargo and films. But the weak global economy and Japan's own protracted recession made it unlikely that Tokyo would take the trade barriers down any time soon.

By late 1995, the Japanese economy had been stagnant for four years; real estate prices were continuing their plunge and many industries were suffering from enormous excess capacity built up during the speculative bubble of the late 1980s—about 30 percent in the huge automobile industry. The Nikkei stock index had tumbled 60 percent below its peak. And notwithstanding continued adherence to the principle of lifetime employment, the official unemployment rate had crept up to 3.2 percent.

But the greatest immediate threat lay in the shaky Japanese financial system. During the bubble, Japanese financial institutions made huge real estate loans. Deregulation added to the frenzy. Against a backdrop of increased diversification and global involvement, the financial institutions had insisted they needed more freedom to compete with their opposite numbers overseas. Starting in 1988, the Ministry of Finance allowed banks and credit unions to set their own interest rates. After the collapse of stock markets and the sharp fall of land prices, Japanese companies' financing costs rose sharply, depriving them of their competitive advantage over foreign manufacturers.

On top of the credit crunch came a series of bank failures—including that of the second largest credit union in the country in August, 1995—which threatened to wipe out the funds in Japan's Deposit Insurance Corporation, the Japanese version of the U.S. FDIC. Although the Japanese believed the government would guarantee their money, the failures aroused widespread fear in the international financial community that further defaults could affect liquidity in banks around the world and trigger a global banking crisis. Because Japanese banks maintained large holdings of U.S. Treasury bills and other American assets, the Federal Reserve Board moved quickly to devise a rescue plan to infuse funds into Japanese banks should they run short of money, using the holdings as collateral.

In September, 1995, the Bank of Japan announced a cut in its discount rate to a record low of one-half percent. This was followed by the government's $160 billion spending and loan package. However, the package, like the six before it, was a patchwork, reflecting a Ministry of Finance torn between a desire to pull the country out of recession and an unwillingness to exacerbate a budget deficit equal to 4.5 percent of gross domestic product. (By contrast, the U.S. budget deficit equaled roughly 2 percent of American GDP.) Consistently, the ministry resisted political pressure to use the big fiscal stimulus of a tax cut.

A New Future?

The foot-dragging of the LDP-Socialist government could not hold back the gradual liberalization of Japanese society. Thanks to foreign pressure, especially from the United States, tariffs have been lowered on most imported manufactured goods and considerable improvements have been made in the Japanese distribution system. Today, imported goods are no longer luxuries beyond the reach of average Japanese consumers. Imported wine, beer, and liquors are available at prices competitive with domestic goods. More foreign businesses are finding ways of cracking Japanese markets. The government itself has negotiated several trade agreements with the United States and other countries, notably a January, 1995, accord opening Japanese public and private pension funds to foreign firms.

For their part, Japanese big businesses have begun to recognize that Japan has come to the end of its period of explosive growth, and that the old myths of Japan, Inc. will not help them deal with the new realities. In an age of slow growth, the old solution—expand, expand, expand—will no longer work; they have had to learn the meaning of downsizing. With even giant automakers moving to close major factories, the lifetime employment system has itself gradually come into question, as distressing as this is to a population that has come to feel entitled never to be laid off. Rumors of possible layoffs at major companies have sent shockwaves not just through the ranks of employees but through the entire society. Although most big businesses have managed to avoid a frontal assault on the system, they are dismissing part-time workers (generally women) en masse, encouraging early retirement, and freezing new hiring, particularly of female college graduates.

Pressure on Japanese manufacturers has grown as the yen's appreciation dampened demand for Japanese products overseas. At the same time, steep production costs, the inefficient domestic distribution system, and excessive regulations have made Japan less hospitable to manufacturing. Raising fears that Japanese industry is "hollowing out," many Japanese companies have transplanted manufacturing to lower-cost nations, especially in Southeast Asia, where cheap labor is readily available. In October, 1995, the Sony corporation became the first Japanese electronics giant ever to announce that it would stop exporting Japanese-made color television sets. In addition, lower-priced imports have intensified industrial competition, which has in fact delayed the country's recovery from the current recession.

The persistence of the Japanese trade surplus, reflecting in part a shift in exports from finished goods to parts and equipment, has forced the government to seek ways of encouraging imports.[6] Thus MITI's overseas offices, JETRO, which were originally established to promote Japanese exports worldwide, now vigorously help Japanese companies import foreign goods. Such efforts also point to Japanese policymakers' desire to stave off rising protectionist sentiment around the world.

In fact, the budding reform movement did not die when the

Socialist-LDP coalition retook power in June, 1994. On the contrary, anti-establishment and particularly anti-bureaucratic sentiments remained strong throughout the country. The inept governmental response to the January, 1995, Kobe earthquake, as well as to the poisonous gas attacks that began in 1994 and continued through 1995, shook Japanese confidence in the principle that "central government knows best." Two former television personalities with strong anti-establishment platforms won the gubernatorial elections in Tokyo and Osaka, defeating career bureaucrats running with impressive credentials. In July, 1995, the reformist New Frontier Party made a strong showing in upper house elections, confirming popular discontent with stagnant LDP-Socialist rule.

Where is Japan headed? It is hard to imagine the country resuming its postwar mercantilist course, even if it wanted to. More likely, continued engagement with the rest of the world, on the part of both government and business, will slowly move Japan closer to its economic peers in the West. The revisionist assumption that Japanese capitalism is *sui generis* and must remain so fails to reckon with the nature of the animal—and runs the risk of undermining prospects for economic cooperation. But that is no prescription for Western passivity in the face of continued Japanese economic discrimination; external pressures will still be needed to support the internal forces for change.

In any event, there is no reason to suppose that Japan can continue to play its postwar mercantilistic role without provoking retaliation from the United States and other countries. Such retaliation would be a severe blow to the future development of the Japanese economy. Japan's economic success has depended on the relative openness of world markets to its exports and investments, on Western passivity toward its huge trade surpluses, and on the political tolerance and protection of Japan by the United States during the Cold War. The end of the Soviet threat, compounded by rising concerns about global economic weakness and the imbalance in trade, has radically changed the environment in which Japan's drive for economic expansion worked effectively for four decades. There are signs that Japan recognizes the dangers it faces in overstaying a policy that has had its day.

SEVEN

·······································

Whither Northern Europe?

*Jonas Pontusson**

$\int$ ince the end of the Cold War, the new laissez-faire advocates have taken aim at the welfare state, consigning it to the dustbin of history as an unacceptable halfway house between socialism and the free market. In the considered opinion of House Majority Leader Dick Armey, the result of welfare-state expansion in Western Europe, as in the United States, has been "a stagnant economy, high and persistent unemployment, and little incentive to further achievement." But Armey takes comfort that "even our European friends, the inventors of the welfare state, are themselves getting on board the Freedom train."[1]

There is no better way to understand welfare-state capitalism, and the nature of the recent changes to which Armey alludes, than to look at Germany and its small, affluent neighbors: Aus-

*Jonas Pontusson is Associate Professor of Government at Cornell University.

tria and Switzerland to the South; Belgium and the Netherlands to the West; and Denmark, Norway, and Sweden to the North. For these are the advanced capitalist countries where the welfare state has reached its fullest development. To Armey and other laissez-faire advocates, it seems, all capitalist economies are essentially the same; they differ primarily in terms of the extent to which the welfare state intrudes on the market allocation of resources. However, the welfare state—understood as the public provision of social benefits—is but one way of distinguishing between the "social market" economies of Northern Europe and "free market" economies typified by Britain and the United States.[2]

It is unquestionably true that in Germany and its smaller neighbors, there has been a shift towards the free-market model in recent years. The questions before us are the reasons for and implications of this shift. Is Northern Europe following in the footsteps of Britain and the United States, as Armey would have it? Or does the shift merely represent an adjustment within an essentially stable system, shifting the balance of decisionmaking away from labor toward business, without altering the basic social contract? There is no simple answer to this question, but the following analysis suggests that the social market economy is not as dead a capitalist option as the enthusiasts of laissez-faire would like us to believe.

How the Social Market Economy Works

The social market economies of Northern Europe derive their distinguishing features both from their original pattern of industrialization and from post-World War II political developments.

Compared to Britain and the United States, these economies

were, on the eve of the Industrial Revolution, more agrarian and less commercialized. Private wealth was less concentrated and, above all, less capable of being mobilized to finance industrialization. As a result, Britain got a head start, and its industrial dominance in the nineteenth century in turn shaped the industrialization of Northern Europe. (Because of geographic barriers and the size of its domestic markets, American industry was less directly affected by British competition.)

In the industrialization of Germany, equity markets were far less important than banks, which played a crucial role in mobilizing dispersed savings by taking deposits and engaging in long-term lending. With the Netherlands as the most notable exception, this pattern holds generally for the social market economies, and its implications for corporate governance are still in evidence. The risks involved in long-term lending led the banks in these countries to take an active interest in the affairs of their corporate customers and they continue to do so, commonly insisting on the right to be represented on boards of directors. Through a variety of mechanisms, banks often control major equity stakes in their corporate clients as well.

The role of banks represents only the most well-known manifestation of a broader pattern of "organized" or "coordinated" capitalism, which also features cross-ownership of shares between large firms and the swapping of board representatives. In addition, there are long-term subcontracting relationships between firms that clearly violate the logic of pure market forces. As in Japan, cooperation and trust play an important role in these relationships, not only between large firms and their component suppliers, as in the auto industry, but also within regional networks of small and medium-sized firms that engage in reciprocal subcontracting.

In every one of the social market economies, the vast majority of firms belong to employer organizations, which engage in collective bargaining on their behalf, and regularly sanction members who fail to abide by the terms of collective agreements. Typically, firms also belong to trade associations that represent the interests of industrial sectors vis-à-vis government authorities and provide a range of services to their members. In two cases, Germany and Austria, firms are required by law to belong to chambers of commerce, which primarily cater to the needs of small business.

The encompassing nature and internal cohesion of employer organizations can be seen not only as a response to the growth of strong unions, but also as a factor contributing to union cohesion. Unionization rates vary a great deal across the social market economies, but even in the least unionized of these countries, Switzerland and the Netherlands, unions represent more than one-quarter of the labor force, as compared to 16 percent in the United States. (Prior to unification, the German figure was 33 percent.) At the other end of the spectrum, unions represent more than three-quarters of all wage earners in Sweden, and nearly three-quarters in Denmark.

Even the least unionized of these countries have long been characterized by highly institutionalized forms of (multi-employer) collective bargaining. Collective-bargaining contracts often stipulate that their terms apply to nonunion employees as well as union members, and government legislation also provides for the extension of collective bargaining agreements to employers who are not themselves parties to the contract. Measured in terms of the proportion of the labor force whose wages and other conditions of employment are (at least in part) determined by contracts negotiated by unions and employer organizations, the scope of collective bargaining varies less than unionization rates, and clearly distinguishes the social market economies as a group. Whereas the percentage of the labor force covered by some collective bargaining agreement is 18 percent in the United States, it ranges from 71 percent in the Netherlands to 98 percent in Austria (with the exception of Switzerland, which lags behind at 53 percent).[3] More so than in other capitalist economies, collective bargaining in the social market economies constrains the ability of individual employers to set wages and other terms of employment.

The dominance of industrial unionism, the concentration of union membership in a relatively small number of national unions, and the absence of major political divisions within organized labor also distinguish the industrial relations systems of Northern Europe. Here the contrast with the British case is stark. Despite a precipitous decline in the 1980s, the British unionization rate remains quite high (39 percent in 1990); yet organized labor in Britain has always been plagued by fragmentation, and inter-union rivalries have undermined its ability to engage in coordinated wage bargaining.

With respect to the welfare state proper, it was Germany that became the first country in the world to adopt a mandatory social insurance system. This happened in the 1880s as an effort to integrate the working class within the existing social and political order after the socialist movement was repressed. In Scandinavia, by contrast, the public provision of social welfare remained highly limited until Social Democratic parties, closely tied to trade unions, established firm control of government power in the 1930s. But while the rise of the postwar welfare state was powered by the growth of unions and electoral gains by parties on the left, it was characterized by broad-based political consensus. Indeed, in Germany, Austria, and the Low Countries, rightist Christian Democratic parties played an important role in passing the formative welfare legislation of the immediate postwar period.

As shown in the accompanying table, high levels of social insurance provision and overall government spending differentiate the small social market economies from most other advanced capitalist economies. (This is less true for Germany; among the small countries, Switzerland again stands out as an exception.) Spending data, however, do not capture the full extent of government measures to protect citizens and communities against the vicissitudes of the marketplace. Social protection also includes a range of government regulations pertaining to working hours, working conditions, vacation time, maternal or parental leave, minimum wages and, most importantly, the terms of severance pay and the conditions under which employers can lay workers off. Although it is difficult to measure precisely the level of

Select Measures of Economic Performance and Government Spending

	GDP per capita (US$) 1990	Social security transfers as % of GDP 1990	Total govt. spending as % of GDP 1990	Govt. spending on educ. as % of GDP 1990–91	Exports as % of GDP 1990	Annual growth of real GDP per capita 1960–90
Austria	20,391	19.9	49.6	5.4	41.1	3.2
Belgium	19,303	22.7	55.2	5.1	74.3	3.1
Denmark	25,150	18.4	58.4	7.4	35.1	2.5
Netherlands	18,676	26.3	55.6	6.3	56.6	2.4
Norway	24,953	19.0	54.6	7.9	44.0	3.2
Sweden	26,652	19.7	61.4	7.7	30.3	2.4
Switzerland	33,085	13.4	30.7	5.0	36.9	1.9
Germany	23,536	15.3	46.0	4.0	32.0	2.6
Japan	23,822	11.5	32.3	4.7	10.8	5.3
Britain	16,985	12.2	42.1	4.9	24.6	2.1
U.S.	21,449	10.8	36.1	5.3	9.8	2.0
• OECD-Total	19,333	15.4	43.8		18.5	2.7
• OECD-Europe	16,731	17.4	48.4		28.7	2.6

SOURCES: Figures on education spending from UNESCO, *Statistical Yearbook 1994* (Paris, 1995); all other figures from OECD, *Historical Statistics 1960–1990* (Paris, 1992).

social protection provided by government regulation of the labor market, most observers agree that this type of regulation is especially pronounced in all the social market economies, including Germany.[4]

Returning to the table, it is noteworthy that the Scandinavian countries top the list with respect to overall government spending, but not with respect to government spending on social insurance programs. Reflecting the dominant role played by social democracy in their formation, the Scandinavian welfare states differ from their continental counterparts by their emphasis on benefits financed out of general revenues, and especially on services directly provided by the public sector. By contrast, the public provision of social welfare in Germany, Austria, and Switzerland has been stratified by occupation, with benefits linked to employment and work performance; the administration of social insurance has been delegated to occupation-based associations and other organizations that are neither strictly public nor private.[5]

Full employment came to be associated with the welfare state in the postwar period and, in most of the social market countries, the problem of achieving price stability under conditions of full employment gave rise to more centralized forms of wage bargaining. In Scandinavia, union representatives and employers began to negotiate economy-wide frame agreements for industry-level bargaining after the war, and this type of "peak-level" bargaining also prevailed briefly in the Netherlands. In Austria, formal bargaining remained at the industry level, but the peak associations and the government assumed an increasingly important coordinating role. Meanwhile, postwar governments went beyond social welfare reforms to enact various legislative measures designed to provide employees and/or unions with rights to participate in corporate decisionmaking (and associated rights of access to corporate records). The most important example of this development is the German "co-determination" legislation, which was introduced by a Christian Democratic government in 1951–52.

Cooperative industrial relations at the firm level also characterize postwar Japanese capitalism, but in marked contrast to the Japanese model, co-determination is mandated by law in most social market economies, and firm-level consultations and negotiations occur within parameters set by (multi-employer) collective bargaining. Because this institutional framework is external to the firm itself, it provides labor with a more independent voice and greater bargaining power than in Japan.

Finally, the social market economies are distinguished by substantial public investment in public education and laws that encourage private investment in human capital. As the table shows, the Scandinavian countries devote a considerably larger share of gross domestic product (GDP) to public education than Britain and the United States, and Japan as well. In Social Democratic Sweden, the egalitarian thrust of postwar educational reforms brought vocational training into comprehensive secondary schools, and downgraded its importance relative to academic instruction; the Swedes also pioneered government programs to retrain workers affected by structural unemployment. In Germany, to be sure, public spending on education is substantially lower, but this reflects the fact that a large proportion of German teenagers go into apprenticeship-based vocational training programs that are largely paid for by employers and administered jointly by unions and employers.

To summarize, the social market economies share five core features:

- business coordination by banks, trade associations, and other private actors;
- more or less economy-wide (but not necessarily centralized) wage bargaining;
- social protection in the form of government regulation of labor markets, as well as transfer payments and services provided by the welfare state;
- cooperative industrial relations at the firm level; and
- a strong commitment to public education and worker training.

Other advanced capitalist countries display at least one of these features—Japan with respect to business and cooperative industrial relations, Britain with respect to public provision of social welfare, and France with respect to public education. But only the social market economies of Northern Europe combine all five into a coherent whole.

Among these economies, we can distinguish between Scandinavian and Germanic models. Simply put, the Scandinavian model has gone farther in redistributing income, a policy achieved through centralized wage bargaining as well as through social welfare programs. In 1985, according to a recent OECD study, the Swedish wage earner at the tenth percentile earned 52 percent of the salary of the wage earner at the ninetieth percentile. For (West) Germany, the figure was 38 percent; for the United States, 18 percent.[6] However, what distinguishes the social market economies as a group is not wage compression but wage standardization across firms and sectors. Egalitarianism represents a distinctly Scandinavian take on the social market economy. Altogether, it is not the redistribution of income, let alone wealth, that marks the social market economies, but rather a generous and comprehensive social safety net.

Postwar Growth

The performance of the social market economies in the postwar period poses a challenge for laissez-faire enthusiasts like Dick Armey and Newt Gingrich, who apparently believe that welfare spending and other forms of social protection inevitably lead to inefficient allocation of resources and undermine economic growth. The social market economies of Northern Europe all figure among the world's most affluent nations. As shown in the table, five of the eight had a higher GDP per capita than the United States in 1990, and every one of them had a higher GDP per capita than Britain. More to the point, all but one (Switzerland) averaged higher annual growth rates of real GDP per capita than Britain and the United States between 1960 and 1990. The table also shows that the social market economies of Northern Europe have been particularly dependent on international trade. Germany is the most export-oriented of the large OECD economies, and the small social market economies are more export-oriented than Germany. Although the social market economies did not grow as rapidly as Japan after World War II, clearly they passed the test of competitiveness.

This empirical record might be reconciled with laissez-faire doctrine by arguing that the social market economies were affluent to begin with, and would have performed even better had they been less "social" in their orientation. At a minimum, social market arrangements did not seriously inhibit growth and competitiveness in the postwar period. Yet could it be that they actually contributed to growth and competitiveness?

Many scholars contend that high levels of unionization and centralized wage bargaining actually facilitate the wage restraint necessary to maintain price stability and international competitiveness under conditions of full employment.[7] They argue that wage restraint represents a collective-action problem for workers: While all are better off if they exercise restraint, it is not in the interest of any individual worker to do so. Thus, unions that represent a small percentage of the labor force will always be tempted to take maximum advantage of their bargaining power, but those representing a larger percentage of the labor force must take into account the inflationary consequences of their wage demands. National union leaders are more likely to recognize this imperative than those at the regional or local level.

As some proponents of this line of argument suggest, it might be that the same outcomes would occur if there were no unions at all, and wages were set entirely by market forces; but this is not a realistic scenario in Western Europe. The crucial point is that coordinated wage bargaining has enabled the Northern European countries to avoid the British dilemma of strong yet fragmented unions bargaining at the local level—the worst of all possible worlds from the standpoint of wage restraint.

As noted above, coordinated wage bargaining has taken more or less centralized forms in the social market economies; but in all these countries, the broad scope and institutionalized character of the bargaining has served to link wage developments across sectors, enabling export-oriented industries to assume leadership in wage formation. In the less centralized cases, such as Germany, central banks and employer organizations have played an important role—in effect, taking some of the pressure off the unions. Again, the contrast with the British experience is stark: Because of the lack of employer coordination, responsibility for wage restraint fell entirely on the shoulders of British unions in the 1960s and the 1970s. Even the most cohesive union movement would have had difficulty delivering wage restraint under these conditions.

Social market arrangements may also contribute to economic efficiency and growth through worker training and other investment in human capital.[8] Skill formation constitutes a classic collective goods problem for employers: All employers need skilled workers, but the threat of poaching by other employers makes it irrational for any individual employer to invest in training his or her labor force. The free market economy is likely to give rise to corporate training schemes that emphasize narrow, firm-specific skills, thereby creating an undersupply of general skills.

Japanese employers overcame this problem by agreeing among themselves to hire new employees only at entry-level, and effectively enforced the agreement through trade associations and other forms of employer coordination. In Western Europe and the United States, strong unions and societal conditions (including lack of employer coordination in Britain and the United States) precluded this type of labor-market segmentation. The social market economies solved the problem by combining public education and training, public subsidies to private training initiatives, and union-employer cooperation in administering training programs.

Wage standardization may also come into play by constraining the ability of employers to use higher wages to poach one another's workers. Indeed, employers who are unable to compete for labor by offering higher wages may instead do so by offering training and career opportunities. Thus, wage standardization makes it not only possible but necessary for employers to invest in their labor force. Similarly, institutional factors that inhibit employers from laying off workers during economic downturns might be seen as mechanisms that force (or entice) them to invest in worker skills. Unemployment is not only a waste of currently productive resources; to the extent that the unemployed lose some of their productive capacity over time, unemployment represents a long-term loss of productive potential.

In a comparable vein, the economist Peter Katzenstein has argued persuasively that welfare spending and other forms of social protection serve to compensate workers for losses they experience as a result of changes in the world economy, and that the existence of a comprehensive social safety net has played a key role in securing societal acceptance of continuous economic adjustment to world-market conditions (in particular, the phase-out of employment in low-wage industries).[9] When the Swedish Social Democrats launched a public system of occupational pensions in the late 1950s, they argued that the existing system of employer-organized pension schemes not only provided inadequate and unequal pension coverage, but also created disincentives for employees to move from one firm (or sector) to another. By rendering employees less dependent on particular employers, public pensions would promote labor mobility, and hence economic efficiency and competitiveness.

The logic of this argument might well be extended to other welfare state programs, but it obviously does not apply to government regulations that make it more difficult (or costly) for employers to shed labor. Still, as the Japanese system of lifetime employment shows, employment security may enhance the willingness of workers and their unions to embrace efficiency-improving changes within firms. Arguably, employer-union co-determination has also played a significant role in promoting flexible adjustment to international market forces within firms.

Let us turn, finally, to corporate finance and governance. It has often been observed that dependence on equity markets encourages American and British firms to pursue short-term profit maximization, and to pay out a large portion of their profits in dividends to shareholders. By contrast, bank-dominated systems of corporate finance enable firms to reinvest their profits, and to make investments with long-term payoffs. The social market economies' approach to corporate governance may also have contributed to competitiveness through product specialization. According to the economist David Goodhart, "It is no coincidence that the big three [German] chemical companies— Bayer, BASF and Hoechst—have developed areas of product specialization that prevent direct domestic competition." Goodhart emphasizes that these firms face intense competition in world markets, in the absence of which such coordinated product specialization would simply represent a form of collusion, with negative consequences for efficiency.[10]

Whether or not business coordination promotes competitiveness in general, there can be no doubt that banks have played an important role in managing sectoral crises in the social market economies, organizing the consolidation of declining sectors, such as steel and shipbuilding, and providing for the phase-out of employment on "socially acceptable" terms. In many cases, these private-sector arrangements have reduced the pressure on the state to provide social protection. None of these arguments is meant to imply that social market institutions are in principle more efficient than free market institutions. In the abstract, free labor markets may yield more efficient outcomes than coordinated wage bargaining. But it makes little sense to discuss political-economic institutions in this way. The important question is how the institutions perform in a given societal context. For example, the problem of securing societal acceptance of economic adjustment to international market forces will only arise if societal groups are able to resist the adjustment. Here, a compelling case can be made that social market institutions have promoted growth and competitiveness in postwar Europe. There are good reasons to suppose that institutional practices inspired by free-market doctrine would have performed less well.

The Shift to the Right

Under the leadership of Margaret Thatcher, the British Conservatives in the late 1970s broke decisively with the postwar consensus in the late 1970s and 1980s. Commonly likened to the "Reagan Revolution" in the United States, the Thatcher Revolution entailed a series of reforms designed to roll back the state, curtail union power, and unleash market forces. On the macroeconomic front, the shift from Keynesianism to monetarism meant that the government would henceforth treat the fight against inflation as its top priority, and essentially resign any direct responsibility for the level of employment.

Though American and British conservatives were more strident in advocating the free-market approach, the center of political gravity in Northern Europe was also shifting to the right. Already in 1973, tax revolts at the polls rocked Danish and Norwegian politics. With the sudden emergence of maverick anti-tax parties, the established parties of the center-right were compelled to adopt a more critical view of the welfare state that they had helped build. The Danish and Norwegian Social Democrats subsequently recovered electorally, and were heading up coalition governments in the early 1990s, but had not fully regained the political dominance they enjoyed prior to 1973.

In 1981–82, center-right coalition governments replaced center-left coalition governments in Belgium, the Netherlands, and Germany. In Belgium and the Netherlands, these new governments imposed fiscal austerity, and pursued Thatcher-like deregulation with a great deal of vigor. Electoral gains by leftist parties brought coalition politics back toward the center later in the decade, but the policy shift of the early 1980s endured. In Germany, the coalition forged in 1981 between Christian Democrats and Liberals remained in power through the mid-90s. Indeed, Chancellor Helmut Kohl managed to hold on to power longer than Margaret Thatcher did—in part because better economic circumstances and political constraints (some of which derive from the federal structure of the German state) led him to shun radical economic reform in favor of a more gradual shift to the right.

Only in Sweden and Austria did the left retain control of the government in the 1980s, but here too, a rightward policy shift took place. Promoting private-sector growth by boosting corporate profits, and curtailing the expansion of the public sector, the Swedish Social Democrats departed from traditional social democratic policy prescriptions. The continuity from socialist to nonsocialist governments was striking: When nonsocialist parties came to power in 1976, they essentially pursued traditional social democratic policies, and when they returned to power in 1991, their pursuit of "system change" built on market-oriented reform measures introduced by the Social Democrats in the 1980s. Though the Austrian Social Democrats avoided currency devaluation in the 1980s—a key component of the Swedish strategy—they too pursued more market-oriented policies, including privatization of nationalized industry.

Retrenchment and Deregulation

To what extent, and in what ways, has this shift to the right affected the institutions and functioning of the social market economy? Except in Norway, total government spending (outlays) as a percentage of GDP declined in all OECD countries from the early or mid-1980s to 1989–90 and, in general, the decline was largest in the countries that were the biggest spenders to begin with. Among the small social market economies, Belgium led the way with government spending falling from a peak of 64.2 percent of GDP in 1983 to 55.2 percent in 1990, followed by Sweden (down 5.3 percent from a peak of 66.1 percent in 1983), and the Netherlands (down 4.8 percent from a peak of 62.3 percent in 1987). The decline was modest in Germany, with outlays per capita falling 3 percent from a 1983 peak of 48.5 percent. (Among the large OECD countries, Britain achieved the largest spending cuts in the 1980s—a 4.9 percent decline from a peak of 47.1 percent in 1984.)[11]

These figures reflect not only government efforts to curtail spending but also the rapid growth of GDP in the second half of the 1980s relative to the preceding ten years. During the global recession of the early 1990s, it became more difficult for governments to cut back, and government spending as a percentage of GDP increased in all OECD countries, actually exceeding its previous peaks everywhere except Britain, Belgium, and the Netherlands. This general pattern holds for Social Security transfers as well as for overall government spending. It is also worth noting that from 1983 to 1993 only two European OECD countries, Britain and the Netherlands, reduced government employment as a percentage of total employment by more than one percentage point.

In short, for all the talk of rolling back the state, the size of the public sector has not been significantly reduced in Western Europe. There are three principal reasons for this.[12] First, government efforts to cut expenditures have been offset by mass unemployment and the aging of the population, which have increased welfare entitlements. Second, the political constituencies that benefit from the welfare state—public-sector employees as well as welfare recipients—are large and well-organized, and have effectively resisted cutbacks. Third, the intellectual underpinnings of the welfare state have proven to be quite durable. Public opinion polls show that core public programs such as Britain's government-run health care system remain highly popular. Radical proposals to scale back the welfare state may even have strengthened public support for it.

This said, it would be wrong to conclude that nothing has changed, or that the future of the welfare state is secure. Faced with political resistance, reform-minded governments have avoided large cuts in basic welfare entitlements, but many instances of entitlement cuts can be cited, often targeted against groups that lack political power. In Sweden, for instance, public unemployment insurance was recently reduced from 90 percent to 75 percent of previous income. Governments have fiddled at the margins of broad-based social programs by reducing cost-of-living adjustments and introducing (or raising) user fees for public-sector services. They have sought budget savings by freezing public-sector employment, holding down public-sector pay, and cutting expenditures for infrastructure.

Reformers inspired by free-market principles have also sought to link eligibility for welfare benefits to active participation in the labor force and, in the case of unemployment and pension insurance, to link benefits more closely to (prior) income from employment. This is perhaps most clear in the Scandinavian countries, which have become less egalitarian and more like the German welfare state. Indeed, in all the social market economies, governments have sought to create incentives for people to work more by shifting the tax burden away from income taxes and reducing marginal tax rates at the upper end of the income scale.

Welfare-state "retrenchment" has gone hand in hand with increased earnings inequality. While mass unemployment eroded the marketplace power of unskilled workers in the 1980s, the position of more skilled wage earners improved. Although this shift was partly offset by the continued reduction of wage differentials between men and women, within-gender earnings inequality increased significantly in most countries.[13] OECD-wide data suggest that a trade-off between wage compression and employment growth emerged in the 1980s: In countries where wage inequality increased, employment grew at a more rapid rate than in countries where it continued to decline or remained constant. In contrast to the 1970s, when expansion of the public sector made it possible to have both employment growth and wage compression, market-led employment growth in private services appears to be closely associated with a widening of earnings disparities.

In the social market economies, the trend toward earnings inequality has also been associated with employer efforts to decentralize wage bargaining, allowing for greater wage differentials and, above all, allowing firms to develop pay systems that reward skills acquisition and individual effort. In Sweden, export-oriented engineering employers turned against centralized wage bargaining in the early 1980s, but the unions resisted, and it took the employers nearly ten years to achieve their objectives. Similar if less dramatic developments occurred earlier in Denmark, Belgium, and the Netherlands. In Germany and Austria, where wage bargaining has always occurred at the industry level, wage contracts have become more flexible, allowing for more local variation. As with public welfare provision, collective bargaining has assumed new forms, and become more sensitive to market forces.

Mass unemployment has weakened the bargaining position of labor, especially unskilled labor, and rendered employers less dependent on national unions to help them restrain wage demands. At the same time, there have been a number of political initiatives to relax government regulation of employment— again, more moderate and cautious versions of Britain's "Thatcher Revolution." For instance, the West German Employment Act of 1985 enhanced firms' ability to award temporary employment contracts. But the fact that German employers have not taken full advantage of this legislation suggests that the thirst for deregulation in the social market economies remains limited.

Although the Thatcher governments of the 1980s failed to cut welfare spending decisively, they succeeded in both rolling back union power and privatizing public housing and state enterprise. In the social market economies (other than Austria), privatization did not become a major issue, for the simple reason that there was very little state enterprise to begin with. Some "creeping privatization" has occurred, for instance in contracting out for cleaning and food services by public health authorities. More importantly, the Northern Europeans followed the British lead in deregulating domestic financial markets and removing controls on capital movements across national borders. These reforms have led to a marked increase in financial speculation and foreign ownership of domestically listed shares. Whatever effects the changing operation of financial markets has on economic efficiency and growth, it is bound to stimulate more "short-termism" in corporate decisionmaking in the long run.

Where, then, does all of this leave the social market economies of Northern Europe? Clearly, there has been a retreat from egalitarianism. Social market principles, however, are not necessarily egalitarian. While the changes described above might be interpreted as the beginning of a long-term erosion in the direction of laissez-faire, they are more accurately interpreted as a recalibration of the balance between markets and social institutions—or, for the Scandinavian countries, a convergence on the German model. Although the German economy has itself become more "market-driven," it has shifted less far in that direction than the British and American economies. Relative to Britain and the United States, the social market economies of Northern Europe remain as distinctive as ever.

The Role of Internationalization

Since the late 1960s, the advanced capitalist economies have become increasingly dependent on trade, as well as more closely linked in other ways. The internationalization of financial markets and the growth of multinational corporations are only the most obvious manifestations of economic integration beyond trade in goods and services.

Free traders to begin with, the social market economies have participated fully in this integration process, as illustrated by their increased reliance on exports. Between 1968 and 1990, exports grew from 16.2 percent to 24.3 percent of GDP for West Germany and, on average, from 33.3 percent to 44.9 percent of GDP for the seven small social market economies. (Over the same time period, export dependence increased from 5.3 percent to 10 percent for the United States, from 21.4 percent to 24.4 percent for Britain, and from 10.1 percent to 10.8 percent for Japan.)[14]

It is widely believed that internationalization constrains the autonomy (sovereignty) of national governments, and generates convergence among advanced capitalist economies. Typically, proponents of the convergence theory hold that deflationary policies and free-market institutions will prevail in the new world economy—that internationalization will force social market economies and other "deviants" to converge on something like the American model, either because of that model's inherently superior ability to allocate resources efficiently, or simply as the result of competition among states in a world economy where factors of production (capital in particular) move freely across national borders. Yet in fact internationalization does not appear to have particularly (or disproportionately) affected the social market economies.

From 1983 to 1993, real GDP grew at an average annual rate of 3.0 percent in the United States, 2.4 percent in Britain, and 2.7 percent in Germany (including East Germany after 1990). Among the seven small social market economies, the growth rate ranged between 1.4 percent (Sweden) and 2.9 percent (Norway), and averaged 2.1 percent. In terms of employment growth, Britain and the United States performed distinctly better than the social market economies. But the performance picture changes if we look at the growth of real GDP per person employed (a measure of overall productivity) during the 1983–93 period. By this measure, both the United States and Britain, with annual growth rates of 1.3 percent and 1.6 percent respectively, lagged behind Germany (1.9 percent) and the small social market economies, which averaged 1.7 percent.

It is also significant that in 1989–93 only two social market economies (Sweden and Switzerland) ran higher rates of inflation than the United States, and only one (Sweden) exceeded Britain. Most importantly, all of the social market economies had positive trade balances in 1990–93, ranging from 0.1 percent of GDP in Germany to 4.7 percent in Norway (averaged over four years), whereas the United States and Britain both labored under sizeable balance-of-trade deficits of one percent and 1.7 percent, respectively. The social market economies may not have done very well over the last two decades, but it is by no means obvious that they have become less competitive than Britain and the United States.

Convergence theory implies that the institutional arrangements and government policies associated with the social market economy have become luxuries that cannot be afforded in an increasingly global marketplace. I have argued to the contrary that these have actually contributed to growth and competitiveness. In the postwar period, the German economy was more trade-dependent than other large economies, and the small social market economies more trade dependent than Germany. If social-market practices were conducive to or at least consistent with the maintenance of competitiveness then, why aren't they now? The convergence theory must show that the world economy has changed in ways that favor free-market institutions.

With respect to trade, the theory would seem to fail. Competitive success in the advanced capitalist countries has increasingly come to depend on having well-educated workers with adaptable skills producing high-quality goods in an environment of cooperative industrial relations. This appears to favor (rather than penalize) producers embedded in social-market institutions.

The internationalization of financial markets, and of capital mobility more generally, suggests a greater likelihood of convergence on the American model. For while the social market economies have been more exposed to international competition than their free-market competitors, most of them have had relatively closed financial markets (Switzerland and the Netherlands being the exceptions). Financial integration has made it more difficult—or, to be precise, more costly—for governments to use deficit spending to pay for the education and welfare programs that enhance productivity and ease societal acceptance of economic change. Because deficit spending threatens to weaken a currency by fueling inflation, international financial markets charge higher interest rates to governments seeking to finance current government consumption. This implies that a greater proportion of government spending must now be financed through taxes—a difficult task given ongoing political resistance to increased taxation.[15]

In a nutshell, the challenge to the social market economies in the 1990s is this. The institutionalized power of unions and other organized interests makes compensatory government spending necessary to achieve economic adjustment. While corporations and citizens are unwilling to shoulder further tax increases, and may even insist on tax cuts, the integration of financial markets curtails the ability of governments to engage in deficit spending. Moreover, the internationalization of financial markets can be expected to stimulate more "short-termism" in corporate decisionmaking, with the possibility of reducing productivity growth and competitiveness.

Domestic Politics

If the economic rationale for abandoning the social market economy in favor of an American-style free-market economy is far from compelling, it is nonetheless true that the countries of Northern Europe, like most other advanced capitalist economies, have been plagued since the late 1970s by sluggish productivity growth and, above all, by sluggish employment growth. Though the rightward shift of government policy has been less pronounced than in Britain and the United States, most of the Northern European countries have looked to public-sector cutbacks and deregulation as the solution to these problems.

Countries are not unitary decisionmakers that choose among political-economic models on the basis of a rational calculation of relative efficiency. The politics of economic policy and institutional reform pivot on the interplay of many societal actors who not only seek efficiency, growth, and competitiveness, but also concern themselves deeply with the distribution of income and power (that is, their standing relative to each other). Arguably, the social-market approach to competitiveness remains as viable as it ever was from a strictly economic point of view. But maintaining or rebuilding the social coalition necessary to support social-market institutions has become politically more difficult.

What constitutes a tolerable level of taxation is a political question, and the upper limits of taxation vary across countries and over time. Rising productivity and real wages made it relatively easy for governments to increase taxes in the postwar period. But since the late 1970s support for additional public-sector expansion among wage earners in the lower half of the income hierarchy has weakened as real wages have stagnated or declined. Meanwhile, better-off workers, whose relative earnings increased in the 1980s, have embraced cuts in government spending and taxes. At least in the British case, there are signs that deteriorating public services have led these voters to purchase private services such as health care, daycare, and schooling that the state provides at lower cost, if not for free. There is every reason to believe that this kind of "welfare-state opt-out" generates demands for tax relief, leading to further public-service deterioration in a vicious cycle of considerable potential significance.

During the 1980s, organized labor lost membership and political influence in most of the social market economies, though much less so than in Britain or the United States. In large measure, this decline can be attributed to the growth of private service employment, and the rise of smaller units of production within the manufacturing sector.[16] At the same time, employer organizations and other political representatives of the business community actively mobilized public opinion against high taxes and government spending; they also took advantage of emerging conflicts of interest among unions, playing off local unions against national unions and private-sector unions against public-sector unions. Organized business has become less willing to participate with governments and unions in the kind of tripartite bargaining arrangements that lie at the core of social market economies. This new outlook reflects the constraints of intensified international competition and the opportunities afforded employers by slack labor markets, but ideology also matters. During the postwar period, business learned to live with the social market economy, and recognized the benefits of doing so at a pragmatic level, but it never embraced social-market principles as an alternative to Anglo-American capitalism. For Northern European businessmen, free-market ideology retains much of its instinctive appeal.

The role of the European Community—now the European Union—deserves to be mentioned briefly in this context. Over the last decade, parties and unions on the left and Northern European governments irrespective of partisan composition have tried to persuade the European Union to legislate a minimum floor of social protection and labor-market regulation to prevent a process of competitive deregulation or "social dumping." The 1991 Maastricht Treaty included a "social chapter" that extended the Union's legislative authority in this area, but Britain opted out and most governments subsequently retreated from its ambitious vision. What is more, the European Union's Single Market program undercuts the ability of member states to regulate their economies in such important areas as the control of capital movement and foreign ownership. Indeed, political integration may ultimately constrain the social market economies more than economic integration, especially because it is easier for the European Union to deregulate than to require members states to take action. Yet the future of the Union remains open, and deeply contested. In the end, domestic politics in the large member states will determine the outcome of the contest between free-market and social-market visions of European integration.

The manifest failure of the British Tories to consolidate public support for a free-market agenda in the 1990s suggests that the ascendancy of free-market ideology in European domestic politics may have reached its zenith. In this regard, the Labour Party's new programmatic commitment to the idea of the social market economy is as noteworthy as its spectacular rise in public opinion polls. A Labour victory in the next British election could prove to be a critical moment in recreating the social market economy as the distinctive model of European capitalism.

And why not? Scandinavian-style egalitarianism may have exhausted itself, but the core features of the social market economy leave room for a range of distributive outcomes, and do not necessarily require continued expansion of the public sector.

German unification seems to have had the effect of pushing the German Christian Democrats back toward the political center, emphasizing national solidarity and the extension of West German institutional arrangements to the East rather than radical institutional reform. Even European conservatives find the social polarization characteristic of contemporary American capitalism unpalatable, and there are good reasons to believe that such polarization undermines long-term economic prosperity.

EIGHT

···

Military Spending as
Industrial Policy

Leonard Silk and Mark Silk

I n recent years, few government activities have drawn such
undisguised contempt from American conservatives as industrial policy, or the promotion of private enterprise after the
manner of the Japanese Ministry of International Trade and Industry. Pointing to Clinton administration programs to spur advanced civilian technology and the development of a cheaper,
more fuel-efficient automobile, Dick Armey calls industrial policy a "misguided and often corrupt" effort to pick winners and
losers in the market place: "Proponents of industrial policy nor-
mally talk of 'private-public partnerships to promote the industries of tomorrow,' but usually it turns out to be a give-away to
the industries with the most political clout—often the industries
of yesterday."[1] In 1995, the new Republican majority in Congress
sought not only to strip the federal budget of a range of Clinton-
inspired industrial-policy programs but also to get rid of the

entire Department of Commerce, a Theodore Roosevelt-era creation responsible for, among other things, promoting American
business through loans and international lobbying.

But long before "industrial policy" had a name to label the
process by which government could use its resources to aid
the national economy by protecting, guiding, and strengthening
particular industries, there was a powerful instrument used to
achieve those objectives: military spending.

In 1946, General Dwight D. Eisenhower outlined his proposals
for keeping the military in a state of preparedness. It was important, Eisenhower thought, for the armed forces to be able
to tap industry and the universities for the talent needed for
comprehensive military planning; to do this, they should let
contracts for help in planning rather than merely contracting for
equipment, as had been true in the past. And after the contracts
had been let, the scientists and industrialists involved should
have the greatest possible freedom to carry out research and
development as they saw fit.

Eisenhower thought that if the civilian sector were given its
head after being briefed on the basic problems, it would be much
more likely to come up with useful solutions than if the Army,
Navy, or Air Force were to buzz around trying to duplicate,
correct, or amend the ideas the scientists and industrialists were
developing. At the same time, he thought, the military should
see that some of its officers were well trained in the natural and
social sciences through a thorough program of advanced study.
"Officers of all armed services must become fully aware of the
advantages which the Army can derive from the close integration of civilian talent with military plans and development," he
stated.[2]

Fifteen years later, in his famous Farewell to the Nation, Eisenhower expressed radically different views about the relationship of the military to the civilian sector—what he called the military-industrial complex. "Only an alert and knowledgeable citizenry can compel the proper meshing of the huge industrial and military machinery of defense with our peaceful methods and goals so that security and liberty may prosper together," he said, adding: "The prospect of domination of the Nation's scholars by Federal employment, project allocations, and the power of money is ever present and is gravely to be regarded."[3]

This was no last-minute piece of oratory; he had been worrying about the problem for years. In 1956, in a letter to his friend Everett E. Hazlett, Eisenhower complained that the chiefs of each of the military services had their minds on the good of their own services rather than the nation as a whole, so that the total military budget resulting from their aggregate requests was "fantastic." He said that some day the man sitting in his chair would know less about the military than he did—and less about where budget savings could be made: "Let us not forget that the Armed Services are to defend 'a way of life,' not merely land, property or lives," he wrote to Hazlett. "American strength is a combination of its economic, moral and military force. If we demand too much in taxes in order to build planes and ships, we will tend to dry up the accumulations of capital that are necessary to provide jobs for the million or more new workers that we must absorb each year."[4]

In fact, postwar military sponsorship of research and development did much to build upon the technological advances brought about by organized work on military problems during World War II. It was instrumental in creating the postwar "Information Age" celebrated so enthusiastically by Newt Gingrich as the avatar of his laissez-faire utopia. But the dangers Eisenhower warned against also became more deeply embedded with time. In 1987, Murray Weidenbaum, first chairman of President Reagan's Council of Economic Advisers and a former executive at the Boeing Aircraft Corporation, said in an address to the American Economic Association: "The close, continuing relationship between the military establishment and the major companies serving the military establishment is changing the nature of both the public sector of the American economy and a large branch of American industry. To a substantial degree, the government is taking on the traditional role of private entrepreneur while the companies are becoming less like other corporations and acquiring much of the characteristics of a government arsenal. In a sense, the close, continuing relationship between the Department of Defense and its major suppliers is resulting in a convergence between the two, which is blurring and reducing much of the distinction between public and private activities in an important branch of the American economy." [5]

Prime defense companies and their far-flung subcontractors all over the country learned to work behind the scenes and lobby the Pentagon, Congress, and state and local politicians, to insure that their contracts were obtained or renewed. The coalition might better have been called the Military-Industrial-Political Complex, for the local politico was often the strongest influence in keeping military programs alive: There was no better demonstration of former House Speaker Tip O'Neill's famous dictum, "All politics is local." To local communities, military contracts could be matters of life and death, as when President Carter's cancellation of the B-1 bomber just about wiped out El Segundo, California. To prevent such a thing from happening in their states or districts, senators and representatives have fought with all they had to protect a weapons system that keeps a plant or industry in business, even when the rationale for the weapons system is bogus.

The MX Missile

Does military spending drive economic policy in American capitalism? One piece of evidence in support of the affirmative is the story of the MX missile—a travesty of Cold War strategic planning that ultimately involved three administrations, thirty congressional votes, and several changes in justification and plans for deployment.

Originally proposed because of the fear that the existing Minuteman intercontinental ballistic missiles (ICBMs) were vulnerable in their immoveable silos, the MX was to be deployed so that it could be moved quickly among multiple protective shelters and could play a game of Blind Man's Bluff with the Soviet Union's ICBMs. In an effort to demonstrate how vulnerable the Minuteman ICBMs were, President Gerald Ford's Secretary of Defense, James Schlesinger, told the Senate Foreign Relations Committee in September, 1974 that a Soviet first strike could destroy 90 percent of the 1,054 silos. Then, ignoring the fact that U.S. nuclear strategy made the threat of retaliation the only deterrent against attack, Schlesinger went on to say that the danger of the Soviets' striking American cities and killing as many as 95 million people might make a U.S. president hesitate to retaliate.

Although President Jimmy Carter's Secretary of Defense, Harold Brown, concluded that U.S. forces surviving a first strike would be fully capable of retaliation, Carter bowed to pressure and directed that preparations be made to fight a long but limited nuclear war in which the MX would play an important strategic role. In the spring of 1979, with hawkish senators threatening to vote against the SALT II arms treaty, Carter approved a plan to establish 200 "race tracks," around each of which an MX missile would roll at 30 mph among 23 shelters, shielded from prying satellite eyes except at prearranged times to permit verification. All this would require construction of 4,600 shelters and 13,500 miles of roadway.[6]

Soon the stratospheric estimated cost—$33 billion in 1978 dollars not counting the 2,000 warheads—persuaded the Pentagon to "simplify" the basing plan by converting the race tracks into a grid system of straight roads; reducing the size of the shelters; and using an elaborate series of dummy missiles. The new plan just about negated the entire scheme, however, because hooking up a real missile to its launcher would now take several hours, much longer than the probable fifteen-minute warning period would allow. Nor did it appear even to cut the estimated cost, which eventually rose to $120 billion. Meanwhile, the people of Nevada, Utah, New Mexico, and west Texas, where the missiles were supposed to go, grew increasingly inhospitable to the entire enterprise.

By the time Ronald Reagan assumed the presidency, it had become obvious that the 200–missile moveable force was economically and politically unfeasible. In 1982, Reagan proposed that 100 MX missiles be deployed at Warren Air Force Base in Wyoming in what he dubbed a "dense pack." When Congress told the administration to come up with a less stupid idea, a commission run by National Security Adviser Brent Scowcroft suggested that the 100 missiles be placed in existing Minuteman silos along the Wyoming-Nebraska border. Congress approved this concept, though it made a mockery of the original justification for the MX. The Scowcroft Commission admitted as much, but said that going ahead would demonstrate to Moscow that the United States had "the will" to build an effective deterrent.

Congress approved construction of twenty-one missiles, and by 1985 Reagan was pleading for a total of fifty. To win the PR battle, he began talking about how the "Peacekeeper" was needed to close the "window of vulnerability." He finally declared that the MX was needed as a "bargaining chip" at a new round of arms reduction talks in Geneva. Eventually Congress agreed to keep the MX contractors in business with appropriations for a dozen in 1986 and a total of forty to forty-two down the line.

The story of the MX missile can be multiplied with any number of other examples. The ultimate expression of the Cold War military-industrial complex in action was President Reagan's Strategic Defense Initiative, in which contracts to construct a pie-in-the-sky nuclear missile shield for the United States were distributed not only across the states of the Union but also to defense contractors throughout the Free World. During the Bush administration, reports of high-priced Air Force monkey wrenches and toilet seats created public pressure to do something about cost overruns, overcharges, and outright acts of fraud on the part of defense contractors, including some big ones like General Electric and General Dynamics. Verne Orr, the Air Force Secretary, observed, "National support for building military strength has been severely battered by public perception that we pay too much for the goods and services we acquire." But the problem was inherent in the symbiotic relationship of military contractors, high-ranking military officers, and Pentagon bureaucrats; in the common insulation of defense contractors from normal business competition; and in the political support provided by senators and representatives looking after their constituencies' interests and their own re-elections.

The Military Build-Down

As powerful as military-industrial complexes around the world have been, they could not prevent a substantial reduction in defense spending after the end of the Cold War. After peaking in 1987, global military outlays declined an average of 7.2 percent annually over the next six years.[7] The bulk of the reductions occurred in the developed countries, and primarily in the former Soviet bloc. Where once the Soviet Union accounted for 30 percent of the world's total military spending, its successor states have come to account for less than 10 percent. In 1992, Russia and Ukraine slashed their procurement of new weapons systems by about 80 percent and 75 percent respectively; between 1991 and 1993, Russia cut its total military spending by more than half. Between 1988 and 1993, the former Warsaw Treaty Organization states of Eastern and Central Europe reduced military spending by 70 percent in order to undertake economic reforms.

By contrast, Western European states remained wary of cutting too much in the face of political instability to their east and in the former Yugoslavia. The ceilings imposed by the 1990 Treaty on Conventional Armed Forces in Europe (CFE) stayed high, and had little direct effect on military outlays in NATO countries. Overall, military spending in Western Europe declined only one percent per year between 1988 and 1993, as compared to average reductions of more than three percent in the United States. The cuts in the U.S. military budget were themselves very modest, considering that about 60 percent of that budget had been attributable to the contest with the Soviet Union. What the slow pace of reductions in military spending by the capitalist countries reflected was the linkage between national security and economic concerns, for without question, recession and unemployment helped delay arms reduction and limit the size of any peace dividends.

In the developing world, military spending showed wide regional variations. In economically strapped North Africa, it declined more than 7 percent annually between 1988 and 1993; but there were small increases in Sub-Saharan Africa, where violence exploded in countries like Somalia and Rwanda. In Central America, the staging ground for some of the last and grimmest Cold War conflicts, military spending virtually ground to a halt between 1988 and 1993, whereas in South America the annual reductions were less than 4 percent. In the Middle East, heightened feelings of insecurity in the wake of Iraq's invasion of Kuwait and the subsequent Gulf War led countries briefly to increase defense outlays, but they then resumed a downward course that had begun in the early 1980s.

In Asia, military spending rose and was likely to keep on rising. Widespread political uncertainties, especially over possible threats from North Korea and China, led many Asian governments to increase the preparedness of their armed forces. These countries modernized their armed forces through purchases of submarine fleets, advanced aircraft, and air reconnaissance systems.

The International Arms Trade

Stuck with excess capacity, defense contractors today find themselves in an unprecedented buyers' market. Altogether, world arms imports declined from a peak of around $90 billion per year in the mid-1980s to $22 billion in 1993. Nor does this 75 percent decrease fully convey how much more competitive the international arms trade has become, as defense industries in the developed countries seek to expand foreign sales in order to cope with domestic reductions in defense expenditures, and countries in the developing world gear up their own arms production for the sake of their domestic economies. Nothing illustrates the squeeze better than the cases of East and South Asia, which between 1988 and 1993 increased their military spending by 2.3 percent and 2.9 percent per year, respectively. Both regions reduced their arms imports substantially during the same period: East Asia by more than two-thirds and South Asia by 95 percent.

Of course, with the end of the Cold War the ideological basis for the United States and Russia to transfer arms to proxy states evaporated. No longer so willing to give away expensive weaponry, the Americans and the Russians ended up either reducing arms transfers to their former Cold War allies or discontinued them entirely.

Arms exports by the Soviet Union and its primary successor state, Russia, dropped from an average of $23 billion per year during the 1980s to only $2.5 billion in 1992 and 1993. Russia fell to third place (behind the United Kingdom) among arms-exporting states, with the bulk of its sales going to Iran, China, Afghanistan, India, and Cuba. The aggregate sales level was comparable to actual sales during the Cold War; the precipitous decline in exports had to do with the inability of the Russian government to subsidize exports the way the Soviets had. The biggest outlays of the Russian military now go for pensions and to maintain its more than two million military personnel. The Russian Central Bank provides subsidies to its military-industrial complex through the new Ministry of Industry for the sake of avoiding unemployment and retaining skilled workers—to meet the needs of civilian conversions, they hope.

But the United States has cut military outlays far less than Russia, thereby becoming the dominant player in the arms export business. To cite one striking shift, the U.S. share of military exports to developing countries rose from 16 percent to 51 percent between 1983 and 1993, while the Soviet/Russian share dropped from 44 percent to 10 percent. The apparently spectacular performance of American high-tech weaponry during the Gulf War proved to be seductive advertising for U.S. arms contractors; since then, the United States has garnered half the global arms export market. Some observers even believe that the United States can become the monopoly supplier of arms in world markets.[8] Nevertheless, in the shrinking arms market, American military producers have had reason to worry about the loss of orders to foreign competitors.

The countries of Western Europe in 1993 accounted for 32 percent of world arms sales, with the United Kingdom, Germany, France, and Italy representing over 90 percent of the total: Britain exported $4.3 billion; Germany, $1.1 billion; France, $0.7 billion and Italy, $0.4 billion. (A main component in the German figure has been its disposal of military equipment owned by the former East German armed forces.)

In 1993, China was the fifth largest arms exporter in the world, accounting for 4 percent of all military exports and 8 percent of conventional arms sales. Although China wants to earn more hard currency, the reality is that most countries purchase Chinese weapons only because of their inability to buy from other sources, especially the United States. In many cases, Chinese weapons have been transferred on concessionary terms, in an effort to build closer political ties. China has secretly helped several Middle Eastern countries' nuclear weapons programs; it has exported nuclear-related materials to Pakistan and nuclear reactors to Iran. Defying the nonproliferation agreement on missile technologies of the so-called Big Five supplier states—the United States, the Soviet Union, France, Great Britain, and China itself—China has also attempted to ship long-range ballistic missiles to Iran. However, Chinese arms shipments have mostly consisted of fighter aircraft, armored vehicles, and naval vessels. Beijing's main customers are South Asian nations—Bangladesh, Myanmar (Burma), Thailand, and Pakistan. Its efforts to market Chinese weapons in other areas have been hampered by more competitive Russian weapons. The U.N.-sponsored embargo of Iraq, which had been China's primary customer in the Middle East, deprived it of a major revenue source.

Meanwhile, India, Japan, Taiwan, and South Korea are upgrading their already substantial arms production capacities, and Southeast Asian countries are busily trying to catch up. Indonesia has made efforts to develop domestic aerospace and shipbuilding industries; Singapore wants to expand and diversify its defense industry to promote arms exports; and Malaysia and Thailand have moved to develop the capacity to produce high-tech weaponry. These countries are soon likely to join such other arms-exporting countries in the developing world as North Korea, Brazil, Turkey, Israel, Egypt, and South Africa—making the global arms market even more congested, with producers cutting prices further to push sales, largely for the sake of their domestic economies.

The Contract with the Complex

Just after the Gulf War, then-Chairman of the Joint Chiefs Colin Powell remarked, "I'm running out of demons. I'm running out of villains. I'm down to Castro and Kim Il Sung."[9] Within a few years, Kim, the North Korean leader, was dead, leaving only the tottering regime of Fidel Castro in Cuba. But notwithstanding the villain shortage, military contractors worked hard to keep awareness of threats alive and vivid, and to invent new ones. After the 1994 election they found a receptive audience in the Republican-controlled Congress, quickly demonstrating the political limits of the new laissez faire. For here was a form of industrial policy that free-enterprisers would support, Cold War or no Cold War.

To be sure, among libertarian purists the workings of the military-industrial complex were almost as bad as any other exercise in big government. As Jeffrey Gerlach, a Cato Institute foreign policy analyst, put it: "During the Cold War, the presence of a formidable enemy provided at least some rationale for continuing programs of dubious value. However, in an era when significant threats to the United States have virtually disappeared, it is intolerable to continue to justify defense spending on the basis of its alleged economic benefits." Gerlach acknowledged that the military pork barrel rested on America's readiness to put its military might to the service of peacekeeping around the world. The true libertarian position was isolationist: America should be militarily prepared only to safeguard its own vital (economic) interests. Therefore, so long as the United States left the Haitians, Somalis, former Yugoslavs, and the rest of that ilk to their own devices, it could safely cut its defense budget in half.[10]

This, however, was a far cry from the position of Newt Gingrich. In his 1995 manifesto, *To Renew America*, the House Speaker portrays the world as full of "clever countries" that are trying to "learn how to cope with an American military force";

these include Russia, India, China, Libya, Iran, Iraq, and North Korea. And that's not to mention the threat of international terrorism and Islamic fundamentalism. "We have to plan," says Gingrich, "based on the assumption that somewhere there may be an opponent with the courage and determination to test us in circumstances that we have not considered, using systems that we have not invented ourselves." Drawing on the post-Vietnam Republican tradition of portraying the Democrats as soft on defense, Gingrich contrasts the smashing success of Desert Storm with the grinding stalemate of the Korean War: "The decisive difference was the Reagan military buildup of the 1980s as compared with the Truman defense demobilization of the late 1940s." In Gingrich's view, the collapse of the Soviet Union "has actually widened our range of responsibilities and is spreading our forces even thinner across the planet." America should be "frugal" in its military spending, but now that it has the "potential to lead the entire human race," it must recognize that it must shoulder a greater military burden than ever.[11]

A certain amount of local military-industrial politics buttressed Gingrich's internationalist posture. His district northwest of Atlanta is home to a Lockheed Aircraft plant and a major military base (Dobbins) that together poured $2.8 billion of Defense Department money into the local economy in 1994. The Lockheed plant is largely taken up with manufacturing C-130 transport planes, whose business it is to project American military might across the seas; and the plant is counting heavily on the Pentagon's deciding to spend over $8 billion to replace its entire 165-plane fleet with new C-130J models. (Ultimately, Lockheed would like to manufacture one thousand C-130Js, more than 80 percent of which would be sold outside the United States.)[12] Not surprisingly, Gingrich's recipe for defense frugality is focused entirely on limiting Congressional review and reducing Pentagon paperwork and "civilian micromanagement." There's not a word about preventing cost overruns and fraud, or subjecting defense contractors to the discipline of market forces.

All in all, the Republican Contract with America, perhaps reflecting divisions between Gingrich and his less internationalist colleagues, treaded rather gingerly on the defense question. While generally denouncing the Clinton administration for making excessive cuts in military spending, it did not come out in favor of any particular spending level or oppose further base closings. Rather, it promoted a National Security Restoration Act that would prevent "raiding" the defense budget to pay for social programs; maintain a strong NATO under U.S. leadership; and forbid placing American troops under United Nations command.

The last of these betrayed more than a trace of the isolationist impulse that, seventy-five years earlier, had led Republicans to oppose U.S. membership in the League of Nations. The old spirit of Fortress America was likewise apparent in the sole defense program the Contract said it wished to reinvigorate: President Reagan's Strategic Defense Initiative. The Defense Department would be directed to develop "at the earliest possible date" an antiballistic missile system to protect the United States from, "for example, accidental or unauthorized launches or Third World attacks."[13] The multi-billion-dollar SDI bazaar would be open for business again—though given that the danger was now judged as coming from any number of obscure and unforeseen adversaries, the program presumably could never be justified, like the MX, as a "bargaining chip" at some future arms control negotiating table.

When Congress got down to business in 1995, the disparate

propositions advanced in the Contract spawned a more concrete pledge to prohibit any further reduction in U.S. defense spending. In the course of the year, House and Senate appropriations committees moved to increase the Clinton administration's $234 billion budget proposal by nearly $9 billion—most of which was to pay for weapons systems the Pentagon said it did not want. These included additional B-2 (stealth) bombers, the troubled, supposedly radar-evading strategic aircraft whose justification had been dubious even when it was to drop nuclear weapons on the Soviet Union, and which the Pentagon itself now said it didn't want. The real justification, of course, was keeping the B-2 contractors in business.

How far Washington can go in preserving the military-industrial practices of the Cold War is less than clear. The post-Cold War world remains dangerous, and as the Clinton administration and its Republican adversaries both discovered in Bosnia, the pressure to produce a peace backed by American military might may be hard to resist. But popular reluctance to become involved in foreign lands has grown stronger, and could well lead to a scaling back of America's overseas commitments. Among the dangers is an internationalist's nightmare: isolationist withdrawal from the world's ugliest problems combined with the worst kind of industrial policy—a military pork barrel designed to protect American soil against imaginary threats.

Military-Industrial Perils

Despite short-term economic benefits, arms exports have ominous political effects and long-term costs for producers as well as consumers—through wars, internal or external, that destroy lives and property. The United Nations Development Program counted eighty-two armed conflicts between 1988 and 1992, of which all but three took place within the borders of an existing state. Whistling past the graveyard, the *Economist* editorialized that "like the development banks and aid agencies," arms-producing countries "should refuse to help the big military spenders. They will not put an end to the crazy primacy put upon defense spending in parts of the poor world—that will come only with democracy—but they can save some of their taxpayers' money, and perhaps some other people's lives."[14] In fact these countries have done what they could to shore up their arms exports in an effort to maintain employment and satisfy the needs of their military-industrial complexes.

During the period of the Gulf War, the Bush administration did make some gestures toward restricting the flow of conventional arms to the Middle East. In testimony before the House Foreign Affairs Committee in February 1991, Secretary of State James Baker said that the time had come to "take concrete steps" to stem the flow of armaments in the Middle East, and on March 6, 1991, a week after the liberation of Kuwait, President Bush called for arms trade restraint, saying that it would be tragic if the nations of the Middle East were now, in the wake of war, to embark on a new arms race.

On May 29, 1991, in a speech to the graduating class of the U.S. Air Force Academy, Bush unveiled his Middle East Arms Control Initiative, in which he suggested that the Big Five commit themselves to guidelines for arms suppliers. The United States then proceeded to initiate discussions on reining in nuclear and conventional arms exports among the five permanent members of the U.N. Security Council. At talks on arms control in the Middle East in Paris and London in the summer and fall of 1991, the Big Five agreed to seek rules of restraint for conventional arms transfer and to meet regularly to discuss their implementation. On December 1991, the U.N. General Assembly resolved to establish a register of arms transfer by a vote of 150 to 0, with only Cuba and Iraq abstaining.

Iraq, the largest weapons importer in the 1980s, did disappear from the arms market, thanks to the U.N. embargo. Washington's "dual containment" policy also checked arms sales, particularly high-tech products, to Iran. In actuality, however, little or no progress was made in curbing conventional arms exports to the Middle East, and America's Gulf allies went ahead and made heavy purchases of arms, mostly from their principal benefactor. And generally, U.S. policy since the end of the Cold War has tilted away from limiting the conventional arms trade. The tilt was epitomized by the transformation of the State Department's small Office of Munitions Control into an expanded Center for Defense Trade, which along with the Commerce Department has played a key role in facilitating American arms exports. The Clinton administration also acted to reduce restrictions on arms exports by "streamlining" the bureaucratic review process and liberalizing trade in dual-use technology—that is, technology with both military and civilian applications. These changes in policy flew in the face of the administration's crisis-based opposition to lifting the arms embargo against the former Yugoslavia prior to the signing of the Dayton peace agreement in 1995.

Here, memory of Saddam Hussein's importation of dual-use technology to build up his military machine weighed less heavily than the argument that maintaining existing restrictions only harmed U.S. economic interests. As Democratic Rep. Sam Gejdenson, whose Connecticut district includes some prime defense contractors, said during Congressional hearings on the subject,

"[A]dvances in technology have outstripped the ability to control dual-use equipment. Much of what we are making is too small, too good and too commonly available for us to have any realistic expectation of keeping it out of the hands of dangerous countries."[15] The arms-export deregulation had its effect. Although actual U.S. arms sales declined from $15.4 billion in 1989 to under $10 billion per year from 1990 through 1993, arms sales *agreements* in 1993 jumped by $15 billion, portending expanding exports in years to come.

Governments often seek to justify large arms sales as an instrument of foreign policy, such as to reach or maintain a balance of power, even when these same objectives might be achieved far more cheaply and far less dangerously by arms control agreements. Moreover, exporting arms sometimes works against nations' own political interests. The fall of the Shah of Iran left massive amounts of American weaponry in the hands of the virulently anti-American regime of the Ayatollah Khomeini. Similarly, a large portion of the weapons delivered to anti-communist Afghan rebels wound up in the hands of anti-Western Islamic radicals and helped to arm their "floating" armies. Western arms manufacturers have contributed to the development of arms industries in the developing world by transferring not only weapons but military technologies as part of their "offset" agreements with Third World countries.

The pursuit of immediate economic gain through arms sales on the part of Western countries may also harm their long-term economic and security interests. There is heightened danger to world peace and economic development if military programs, economic objectives, and foreign policy are scrambled—with the military-industrial-political players doing the scrambling. The commercialization of national security and foreign policy not only diverts domestic resources from more productive use but results in global poverty and slow or negative growth. It is an especially dangerous case of what might be called capitalist myopia.

NINE

·········· ·········· ·········· ·········· ·········· ··········

The Future of Capitalism

Leonard Silk and Mark Silk

I n the ideology of the American right today, what makes for national prosperity is some combination of laissez-faire economics, minimalist democratic government, traditional religion, and middle-class virtues.

"We must," declares Newt Gingrich, "rethink all the things that inhibit our ability to compete: regulation, litigation, taxation, education, welfare, the structure of our government bureaucracies."[1] Democracy and capitalism "work together," says Dick Armey, and both derive from a higher power: "We have been called to Freedom by God. I think the free market arose from that calling."[2] In the view of the Christian Reconstructionist David Chilton, "Godly cultures have the 'Puritan work ethic' deeply ingrained into their natures, and this has notable effects in economics: rising productivity, rising real wage rates, and accelerating dominion over every area of life. But ungodly men

... are slaves by nature.... The unbelieving culture thus gravitates toward statism and socialism."[3]

And then there is the claim of Irving Kristol, father of neoconservatism, that any attack on hard work, the family, or religion is necessarily an attack on capitalism, for "[i]f you delegitimate this bourgeois society, the market economy—almost incidentally—is also delegitimated." Indeed, Kristol takes to task none other than the founder of free-market thinking, Adam Smith, for imagining (Enlightenment intellectual that he was) that cultural attitudes and religious opinions are matters of personal taste rather than the necessary foundation of the economic system: "For two centuries now, Western civilization has been haunted by this stupendous error of judgment, with the result that today, even as a market economy is accepted as superior to any other, at least in principle, the bourgeois society on which the market economy is based is being challenged with unprecedented boldness."[4]

Free Markets and Other Values

Such claims are, at the very least, exaggerated. As we have seen, highly regulated and/or heavily taxed countries like Japan and the social market economies of Northern Europe have fared very well during the past half century—despite their relatively ungodly cultures and thanks in no small measure to the very un-laissez-faire protections and guarantees they have afforded their economic enterprises and citizens. In China, as well as in most of the other rapidly advancing countries of East Asia, capitalist economic progress has come about in the absence of democracy, and at times amidst considerable repression.

Notwithstanding the views of today's Christian Right, godly

cultures have long been ambivalent about the pursuit of wealth; moreover, while both Western and Eastern religions have often accorded the highest spiritual value to those who forswear private property in favor of a communal ("socialistic") lifestyle, there has been no shortage of nonbelievers who have enthusiastically embraced "Puritan" work habits. That the pursuit of private vices leads to public economic benefits was a commonplace in Adam Smith's time, and is no less true now than then. The genius of the market, like the genius of democratic politics, is that both are capable of transforming some of the less attractive human attributes—the hunger for wealth, the thirst for power— into servants of the public weal.

None of this is to suggest that there are no positive correlations between national prosperity and free markets, democracy, and traditional religious and cultural values. The preservation of an effective and dynamic economy may well be difficult without some measure of democratic governance; conversely, maintaining a healthy democracy is likely to be difficult without some measure of economic freedom. But the correlations are loose, shifting, and at times inverse. Clashes among desired ends and the means of achieving them—between morality and liberty, liberty and equality, equality and efficiency, efficiency and quality of life—cannot be escaped, and every nation must work out its own ways to resolve them.

Optimists maintain that capitalism will eventually bring greater political freedom in its train—that, as has happened in Taiwan and South Korea, economic advancement in China will not result in a passive and quiescent population but one that sooner or later demands freedom of speech and freedom from fear of oppression by the state. But cause and effect could just as easily work the other way, leaving an economy undermined by authoritarian rule. In any event, political freedom will not come about on its own as the result of some ineluctable economic process; it takes pressure, and the will to make it happen. Above all, the abuses and cruelty of one-party dictatorship need to be combatted for their own sake, not because they could adversely affect economic development in the long run.

Will the Chinese combination of authoritarian political control and a large and growing capitalist sector provide a better model for the economic development of poor countries than the more democratic political systems of Russia or India? The answer depends substantially on the *goals* that nations, or whoever runs them, seek. If accelerating the rate of economic growth and raising living standards are the only criteria of success, the prize may indeed go to free markets combined with political authoritarianism; but if the criteria of success include not only higher economic growth and living standards but also the safeguarding of human rights and people's feelings of worth and self-respect, the judgment may be that India, Russia, and other democratic societies will ultimately do better in meeting their people's most important wants and needs, including the protection of life itself.

Some observers have argued that the United States should not try to force other countries to accept transplantation of a political-economic system for which they have no historical or cultural foundation. They warn of the risk—even to ourselves—of pushing for Western democracy and concepts of human rights, maintaining that this would make economic development more difficult, and even impede the gradual movement toward a functioning political democracy. But others hold that there is an appetite for democracy and freedom among most people, stemming from ancient roots and nourished by resistance to dictatorial control. If the anti-communist revolution in Eastern

Europe reflected resentment of prevailing economic conditions, it drew its strength from popular longing for freedom from oppression. The countries of the Former Soviet Bloc will be weakened if their governments and institutions lack legitimacy, a legitimacy that can only come from winning the support of the people. But the reverse is also true: If their economies fail, these fledgling democracies will also fail—and increase the peril of a revival of conflict with the West.

In the modern age, democracy developed in a struggle against the oppressive structures of the state. Over the past century, however, the evolution of Western democracy is largely a story of how unfettered capitalism and the interests it has served have gradually been restrained in the public interest. It is democratic institutions—including freedom of the press, of popular expression, and of assembly—that ensure that the state acts to safeguard the interests of the people against the failures of the market, and the uncertainties of nature. Where China suffered millions of deaths from famine under communist totalitarianism, India has not experienced mass starvation since it achieved independence after World War II, despite severe droughts and extremes of wealth and poverty. Thanks to a free press that has dramatized the urgency of rescuing famine-imperiled people in different parts of the country, the Indian government has responded in time to head off threatened disasters.

But free markets and democratic institutions cannot, in themselves, guarantee solutions to all the problems of human misery. India is a case in point. Despite faster economic growth in recent years—the result of market liberalization and other economic reforms—the urgent need to focus national policy on healing the abysmal living conditions of the poor was dramatized by the outbreak of pneumonic plague in the city of Surat in September

1994. While the number of recorded deaths was less than one hundred, the plague, because of its horrific history and the speed with which it struck, spread fear throughout the country. It forced the political elite to pay greater heed to the dreadful social and sanitary conditions in which the poor lived, crowded into slums with open sewers and virtually no means of getting rid of human wastes—conditions for breeding plague or other diseases that threaten to infect rich, poor, and middle-class people in all parts of the country.

During the political debate set off by the plague's outbreak, Prime Minister Rao, who led the drive to liberalize the Indian economy, said that the economic reforms of the preceding three years were not enough to bring "genuine prosperity" to the great mass of Indians. India's growth could be dragged down by the maldistribution of the economic benefits of growth and neglect of the masses of poor people.

Hungry, sick, homeless, and illiterate people cannot contribute to economic development and technological and industrial modernization.[5] They are a disgrace for a nation whose affluent and middle-class people are moving rapidly ahead. Those who benefit from marketization and privatization in the developing world cannot ignore those left behind without threatening the entire economic and political system. It is up to the government to make sure that they do not.

The Visible Hand

Experience after World War II showed that the conversion of economies from war to peace, if shepherded by intelligent national and international policies, could bring about enormous economic benefits. Following the most devastating war in history, with many millions dead from the war and many countries lying in ruins, the world enjoyed the longest and strongest period of economic growth in history.

Virtually everyone was surprised by the speed with which the prostrate economies of the industrial world were revived. The underlying knowledge and skills, the habits of work and thought, the structure of industrial organizations, and the economic institutions were still there. "I always thought it was impossible for the German economy to recover," said Theodore Schultz, later a Nobel laureate in economics, who served in the Allied occupation of Germany. "We were dead wrong—British economists, American economists, and for that matter Germans." They had all underestimated the real growth forces in West Germany. The plants and cities that had been destroyed were, said Schultz, "really quite secondary, minor details remedied in very short order."

By contrast, the collapse of communist regimes and economies in Eastern Europe and the former Soviet Union posed far more difficult tasks of political and economic reconstruction in a world much less capable of undertaking them. After World War II, the United States could deal with the external financial requirements for reconstruction without running a budget deficit. In the 1990s, not only was the world's only remaining superpower running big internal and external deficits, but there were doubts that even the Group of Seven largest industrial democracies could collectively provide enough capital for the ex-communist countries, even if they wanted to. And there was little sign that they wanted to.

The problem of capital shortage was only one of the obstacles the former communist states needed to overcome. They had to get rid of the Stalinist economic institutions and the habits and attitudes inculcated by years of sclerotic central planning that stood in the way of economic advance. They needed to learn how to conduct sensible macroeconomic policy; huge budget deficits and loose monetary policies threatened hyperinflation and the collapse of the ruble and other national currencies. They needed to determine in each sector of the economy whether private, public, or mixed ownership best satisfied individual or social needs. Above all, they needed to be able to close down the huge industrial firms that would never be able to compete in world markets. The prevention of unemployment was a major attraction of communism; to facilitate the change to a productive market economy that satisfied people's consumption needs and desire to work, governments had to take the responsibility of creating jobs, and educating and training workers to handle those jobs, lest they grow resentful and restive for a return to the employment security of the old regime. Governments needed to improve the infrastructure both as a means of job creation and for its own sake.

But the economic doctors, in thrall to free-market ideology, declined to follow in the footsteps of post-World War II reconstruction. They gave little thought to nurturing new industrial enterprises and guiding them into the world economy; even less to creating appropriate safety nets to assure citizens that they would not be abandoned during the transition to a stable market economy. The reforms they prescribed neglected the barriers to economic growth posed by the inadequate legal, moral, and institutional foundations for an effective market economy. Strengthening those foundations was necessary to call forth the commitment of foreign capital and direct foreign investment, as well as internal saving and investment. Privatization became a byword of the day, and a lot of transfer from public to private ownership commenced. But privatization did not provide the answer to the most appropriate forms of ownership or control for all industries or functions.

Douglass North, the 1993 Nobel laureate in Economic Sciences, attacked this approach by calling the underlying economic theory "simply an inappropriate tool to analyze and prescribe policies that will induce development." Pointing out that neo-classical economics was concerned with the operation rather than the development of markets, North insisted that "transferring the formal political and economic rules of successful Western market economics to Third World and Eastern European economies is not a sufficient condition for good economic performance."[6] On the contrary, Western economists' lack of concern for the role of government in developing a workable market economy led most Eastern governments to pursue no coherent policies at all. They tried to support existing firms; they tried to control subsidies; they tried to let prices adjust to world prices; they tried to protect domestic users from price increases for energy and other raw materials. These policies, which were mutually incompatible, put the Eastern economies and their people through a harrowing experience, with falling living standards and rising joblessness, social discontent, and hostility toward foreigners or different ethnic groups.

As a result, old communists began to generate considerable electoral appeal throughout the Former Soviet Bloc. Not that politicians like Gennadi Zyuganov, head of the revived Russian Communist Party, publicly advocated a return of dictatorial one-party rule, the abandonment of freedom of expression and civil liberties, or a rejection of private property. But they promised a distressed population respite from the turmoil of the disorderly capitalist present, whether by renationalizing some industries or

limiting the ability of the well-placed few to amass huge for-
tunes. Unfortunately, they too lacked the intellectual where-
withal to manage the transition.

While there is no doubt that communist totalitarianism lost
the Cold War, it is unclear how capitalistic the people of the
former Soviet bloc will want their economies to be. How capitalistic should they be?

Decentralized political-economic systems are far more efficient than highly centralized ones; an authoritarian government
cannot collect or integrate all the information and knowledge
that diverse individuals and groups possess and that can be
integrated through the market and the democratic political process. At the same time, solutions to the diverse economic problems of the ex-communist countries cannot be black and white; a
combination of public support and private enterprise is needed.
While private foreign investment and indigenous entrepreneurial initiative are essential, the visible hand of government will
still be needed for the transition from communism to succeed.
How much it will be needed and in what ways will differ from
society to society, depending on varying cultural and economic
conditions. In all cases, it will be needed to maintain a measure
of respect for law and human rights, without which individuals
will lack the power to protect themselves, to avoid the plagues
of hunger and sickness, preserve their environment, and advance
their separate economic and social interests. In sum, devising
effective government interventions and protections within the
context of a free society is the prime challenge left behind by the
downfall of Soviet communism.

Exit over Voice

That the anti-government tide which swept over the West in the 1980s should have persisted after the end of the Cold War is not hard to understand. Particularly in the United States, anti-communism had been the way to sell otherwise unpalatable federal initiatives, from the Marshall Plan to national highway construction, from massive support for scientific research to foreign aid, from the Korean conflict to the war in Vietnam. With the Cold War over, there was every reason to expect a resurgence of the traditional American preference for small government, a preference that had been effectively held in abeyance since the Great Depression. Yet that is not to say that the desires of the enthusiasts for small government represented good policy for the United States at the end of the twentieth century.

Before the 1994 elections brought the Republican tax-cutters to power in Congress, U.S. tax rates were among the lowest in the industrialized world. In 1992, total tax revenues in the United States equaled 29.4 percent of gross domestic product (GDP), the same as Japan and well below Great Britain (35.2 percent), Canada (36.5 percent), Germany (39.6 percent), Italy (42.4 percent), and France (43.6 percent). Of all the OECD nations, in fact, only Australia (28.5 percent) and Turkey (23.1 percent) had lower proportional tax revenues. Moreover, contrary to the assertions of anti-tax crusaders, taxes have risen only modestly in recent decades; between 1974 and 1993, total government revenues in the United States increased by only 1.4 percent of GDP. Between 1970 and 1994, federal outlays as a proportion of GDP grew from just under 20 percent to just over 22 percent, while the proportion of outlays for government as a whole (federal, state, and local) grew from 29.7 percent to 32.7 percent. All told, government outlays have remained relatively constant in proportional terms since the end of World War II.[7]

If the government sector of the economy has not grown significantly, why do Americans believe the contrary? The answer may well lie in the decline in American living standards. Between 1973 and 1993, real hourly wages fell or remained stagnant for most American workers. The decline was steepest for those earning least—11.7 percent at the twentieth percentile. For median wage earners—those in the fiftieth percentile—the decline was 7.5 percent; and for those in the sixtieth percentile, it was 4.9 percent. Only at the eightieth percentile was there a small rise of 2.7 percent. Nor do wages tell the whole of the story. Between 1979 and 1989, the proportion of American workers covered by employer-sponsored pensions declined from 50 percent to 42.9 percent, while the proportion with employer-sponsored health coverage fell from 68.5 percent to 61.1 percent. Altogether, total private-sector compensation—including wages and salaries, health and pension benefits—declined 8.5 percent in real terms between 1977 and 1994.[8]

But rather than blame employers, Americans appear to have been willing to accept Republican arguments that the fault lies with government. Significantly, male workers have seen their incomes and benefits decline faster than female workers; in relative terms, white men have fared worse than white women, whose share of better-paying jobs has gone up. This may say something about why, over the past few election cycles, white men have been voting Republican in substantially greater proportions than white women.

Is it simply the case that Americans have been sold a bill of goods that has led them to blame the government rather than business or the economy in general for taking the bite out of their standard of living? Perhaps, but public susceptibility to anti-government rhetoric may reflect a deeper shift in attitude.

⌐ According to the economist Albert Hirschman, there are two basic kinds of responses to institutional decline: "exit" and "voice." Exit represents the characteristic approach of the market: If a product declines in quality, the customer simply abandons it for a better one. Voice, by contrast, is the characteristic approach of politics, whether formal or informal: Given defective policies or behavior, individuals speak up to get them changed. Hirschman emphasizes that the two approaches are not mutually exclusive. Disgruntled customers can voice dissatisfaction with products and services; disgruntled citizens can pick up and leave their town or country. Hirschman's argument is that healthy institutions rely on the availability of some combination of both exit and voice.

Not surprisingly, economists—and those who think like them—have a prejudice against voice. As an example, Hirschman quotes Milton Friedman's justification for subjecting public education to market forces by way of school vouchers:

> Parents could express their views about schools directly, by withdrawing their children from one school and sending them to another, to a much greater extent than is now possible. In general they can now take this step only by changing their place of residence. For the rest, they can express their views only through cumbrous political channels.

Hirschman notes the oddity of the economist's belief that exit is a more "direct" way to express one's views than simply expressing them. As for the contemptuous reference to "cumbrous political channels," he asks, "But what else is the political, and indeed the democratic process than the digging, the use, and hopefully the slow improvement of these very channels?" [9]

The rise of anti-government feelings in both the United States and the rest of the industrialized world may be seen as the expression of a popular desire to shift the balance of social decisionmaking from voice to exit—from politics to economics. People appear interested in removing some of the power to address social needs from public institutions and depositing it in the private sector; they would rather be consumers than citizens. This would explain, among other things, why polls show high levels of public animosity to government, even after government has acted to reduce its role in their lives. What citizens dislike is not so much any particular government officials as decisionmaking by collective voice per se.

Why might the American public have shifted its allegiance in the direction of exit? Consider the way of life enjoyed by the middle-class suburbanites who are increasingly determining the direction of the country. Thanks to cable television, video rentals, and the Internet, they can take their entertainment and stay in touch with the rest of the world from within the confines of their homes. The homes themselves are increasingly likely to sit not on a public thoroughfare, but within a private subdivision with rules of design and behavior and amenities (tennis courts, swimming pools) that they buy into or sell out of. They work and shop not downtown or on a courthouse square but in semi-private office parks and retail malls. It is a lifestyle in which the poor and disadvantaged live farther and farther away, and are less and less visible—except on television as the victims and perpetrators of crimes. The most substantial new public edifice is the county jail. Otherwise, the public space seems more and more attenuated, and with it the place of government in their lives.

To be sure, the advocates of laissez faire vigorously deny

wishing to let the poor sink or swim on their own. They applaud private charity and good works, quoting again and again Tocqueville's observations on Americans' recourse to voluntary associations for carrying out all sorts of worthy purposes that in Europe fell to government. In Majority Leader Dick Armey's view, the very idea of using government to bring about social and economic improvement carries "a certain moral despair."

> Society had to be managed, social progress paid for in tax dollars, compassion made compulsory. Each day in America, in our biggest cities and smallest towns, that assumption is proved repeatedly wrong in uncounted, unheralded acts of personal courage, sacrifice, kindness, fidelity, generosity, and idealism. It was the arrogance of politics that brought about many of the divisions that trouble us.[10]

Shrink the role of politics, and the divisions will, presumably, begin to disappear.

Legislatively, the Republicans set out in 1995 to act on this philosophy. Anything that smacked of income redistribution to the poor became an object of attack, including not only welfare but the earned income tax credit that bolstered the wages of the working poor. (Tax breaks for the rich, such as a cut in the capital gains tax, were all right.) The Republicans claimed to be as opposed to "corporate" welfare as to any other government handouts. In practice, those with sufficient money and connections retained a good deal more voice than exit in the halls of Congress. Sugar and peanut farmers managed to hold on to their protections and price supports. When the American Medical Association expressed concerns about doctors' losing income from the Republicans' Medicaid funding reductions, Speaker Gingrich sweetened the pot to win its support. As for private agencies that received federal grants to do good works, House

Republicans made strenuous efforts to forbid them to use their own funds to advocate publicly for their programs. On the regulatory front, corporate interests wrote the language intended to weaken environmental protections and limit the oversight of the Security and Exchange Commission.

By late 1995, there began to be signs that the American people had become skittish about letting the Republicans carry through the most radical experiment in laissez-faire economics ever attempted in the United States. Victories by Democrats in off-year elections in Maine, Kentucky, Oregon, and Virginia showed it was possible to prevail by running against the Republican agenda, or at least that part of the agenda that threatened Social Security, Medicare, and the environment. The immediate effect was to stiffen Democratic spines, and especially the spine of President Clinton, who appeared to conclude that meeting the Republicans head-on would serve his interests better than temporizing.

However, the decline of organized labor left the Democratic Party without a broad-based organization to represent workers and other groups on a wide range of public issues—not only jobs but health, safety, pensions, housing, civil rights, and the environment; each issue tended to develop its own "single-issue" constituency, whether women, gays, blacks, Hispanics, or the elderly. The whole seemed less than the sum of its parts, with no group broad enough to speak for public goods, or for the poor and homeless.

Making the Capitalist Future

With the end of the Cold War, the world confronts not the end of history—that is, the end of the dialectical process of change created by antithetical political-economic systems—but the historically unprecedented challenge of a world of nation-states subject to a virtually all-encompassing capitalist order. How will capitalism play itself out on national, regional, and global stages? Where will capitalist institutions be embedded in free democratic societies and where in authoritarian or totalitarian regimes? What, in short, is the future of capitalism in the ex-communist countries, in the developing countries seeking a better life, in the industrialized countries plagued by slow growth?

From current trends, a full spectrum of possibilities can be discerned: at one extreme, a world that falls back into hostile forms of nationalism and protectionism that cause the global economy to collapse; at the other, a world of increasingly close integration, vigorous economic development, cooperation for building and maintaining peace, and international cooperation to protect the natural environment. Intermediate outcomes between those extremes are more probable, with nationalism and internationalism varying according to pressures on the system and the kind of leadership nations get or fail to get.

With the dissolution of the Cold War's bipolar structure of world power, the industrialized countries of North America, Japan, and Western Europe may be moving toward a "capitalist cold war," with the United States particularly suspicious of Japan's economic intentions and mercantilistic practices. Within Europe, there is strain and mounting resistance, especially in Britain, to creating a more thoroughly integrated union of states. The world economic slowdown, resulting in high rates of unemployment in many countries and sluggish or negative income growth for the majority of people in developed countries, has exacerbated disintegrative pressures.

Paradoxically, such pressures have been strengthened by

growing global integration and competition, with workers and some businesses in advanced countries believing that their special interests, jobs, and incomes will be adversely affected by free trade. There has been some reversion to nationalism and protectionism. President Clinton had a hard fight pushing through the North American Free Trade Agreement (NAFTA) over labor and populist opposition. He encountered further resistance to Congressional ratification of a U.S. commitment, made during the Uruguay Round of trade talks, to a broader General Agreement on Tariffs and Trade (GATT) and a stronger World Trade Organization. Although both the Clinton administration and the Republican leadership in Congress remained committed to free-trade principles, protectionist flames were being fanned by G.O.P. presidential aspirant Patrick Buchanan and maverick third-party populist Ross Perot, as well as by the pro-union left. Embracing a rising nativism, the Republican Party enthusiastically promoted legislation to enforce new restrictions on immigration, and succeeded in limiting government benefits even to tax-paying legal immigrants.

⌐ Working against these disintegrative forces is a widespread recognition, especially by many leading business corporations, that open markets and a free flow of capital, technology, and knowledge are vital to the future of the businesses themselves and to national and world economic growth. An open world economy is also a powerful means of promoting regional and world peace, in the face of dangers of aggression posed by authoritarian nationalism.⌐

Capitalist states, portrayed by Lenin as inherently and aggressively imperialist, have abandoned the hunt for political empire—territorial acquisition and control—but remain committed to expanding markets, bigger profits, and lower costs from trans-

national business activities. Capitalist enterprise, while sometimes seeking the support of the state to gain particular objectives (such as access to foreign markets), basically wants freedom
to operate without interference at home and abroad.

Labor and other groups on the left fear that the emerging
global economy may mean not only a loss of jobs and income for
themselves, but a loss of power by the nation-state that will
undermine its ability to meet the needs of those groups within
each nation. Such reasoning, however, assumes little or no
growth in total output. The theory of free trade and the law of
comparative advantage hold that the more efficient use of resources resulting from free trade will result in expanded total
world output and hence more production and jobs for each
nation.

That is not to say that every working group or industry will
be better off as a result of more open markets. In the absence of
adequate mobility of labor and capital, nations need to assist
the adjustment process through education, training, investment,
transportation, housing, and other programs. Contrary to contemporary right-wing ideologues, economic freedom—for companies as well as individuals—does not entail a minimalist role
for government. Ever since the first antitrust law was passed
over a century ago, it has been part of America's public philosophy and practice that the federal government must act to protect
and guarantee that freedom. This is the tradition of the mixed
market economy that has enabled the United States to lead the
world through most of this waning century.

It is this tradition that the laissez-faire radicals have rejected.
Opposed in principle to any effort to redistribute the goods
of society for the benefit of all, naively—or self-interestedly—
wedded to a belief in the omni-beneficence of the invisible hand,

they have capitalized on the anxieties of a middle class living in increasingly straitened circumstances. Promising a society in which citizens can hold on to more of what is "rightfully" theirs, they have committed themselves in practice to weakening the ability of citizens to safeguard their rights in the marketplace. Theirs is a model of capitalism far removed from both the mainstream of economic thought and the history of economic legislation extending back more than a century. It is a measure of the demoralization of American society that it has been allowed to get as far as it has. But it need not prevail.

The goal of enlightened world leadership should be to reinforce capitalist institutions with democratic and moral principles that permit the benefits of economic freedom and growth to be shared more equally among the people of any one nation and among all nations. The great challenge is to translate these abstractions into policies that foster development in the Third World and ease the transition to capitalism in the Former Soviet Bloc. While internal and external deficits seriously constrain the financial aid the United States can provide to countries in transition, this country, counting both its private and public resources, has a great deal of physical, financial, and intellectual capital to contribute—as have the other developed countries of Europe and Asia, together with the International Monetary Fund, the World Bank, and other national and regional development funds.

The need for a stable and expanding world economy extends beyond the pursuit of wealth to the search for peace and the protection of human rights and freedom. Such goals, historically protected only within the borders of a nation state, and often not even there, must now be sought within the context of an emerging but still inchoate global economic and political order. Recovery from the breakup of an old political order can never be easy—and never without risks of ethnic or nationalistic bitterness and internecine warfare. Nations must guard against the danger that such outbreaks of violence in the Former Soviet Bloc could spread to Western Europe, the Middle East, Africa, and Asia. An open, stable, and growing world economy and polity will require governments that are respected and respect-worthy; such governments must heed the rights of all their people, not just those of a privileged class or foreigners whose investments or markets they want. The goals of political freedom and protection of human rights cannot be treated as secondary to the goal of economic freedom and progress.

As we have seen, there are many forms of capitalism, and examples of societies that have successfully combined market economies with significantly different cultural and political values. Creating a more prosperous and humane world does not, *can* not, mean forcing all nations into an identical socioeconomic straitjacket. But during this hazardous transition period, making capitalism work will require them to face up to difficult choices. The coming century offers real hope for peace and global economic development, but the hope will not be realized without the determination and skill to secure the opportunities that lie ahead. For the future of capitalism cannot be extrapolated from current economic trends. The future of capitalism will be determined by nations—working separately, and working together.

Epilogue: The (Political) Economy of Capitalism

Robert Heilbroner*

I t is one of the many oddities of the study most intimately connected with the workings of the social order in which we live that a curious inhibition deters its practitioners from mentioning its name. I am speaking of the reluctance of most conventional economists to use the word capitalism. We hear a great deal about "market systems," "free enterprise systems," and the like, but the one term that gives institutional specificity to our mode of economic organization is curiously absent from the professional literature that analyzes it. Indeed, "literature" may itself misrepresent the situation: An intelligent alien, coming across the *American Economic Review* in the course of visiting our planet, might be forgiven in thinking it a journal of physics.

The reluctance to use the word "capitalism" stems, I believe, from the desire of economists to protect the "scientific" character of their work from being tainted by political considerations.

*Robert Heilbroner is Norman Thomas Professor of Economics, Emeritus, at the New School for Social Research, New York City.

The profession is right, of course, that the term "capitalism" is inextricably political in nature for reasons that we shall look into in this epilogue. But the profession is seriously mistaken in believing that the workings of the system would be less clearly understood if we were to reinstate "political economy," the nomenclature of Smith and Ricardo, in place of the chaste "economics" that became its designation after the publication of Alfred Marshall's text of that name in 1890. Indeed, in the spirit of Leonard Silk, I hope to show that our understanding of the social order in which we live is seriously distorted by a failure to perceive that much of what passes as scientific economics is, in fact, "political" economics, whose unscientific content is all the more pernicious for being unrecognized.

Let us start by outlining the quintessential elements of a capitalist order. This book has already identified these elements as private property, freedom of enterprise, the profit motive, and competition, but I prefer to name three somewhat similar aspects that provide more specific shape and greater life to its behavioral dynamics.

The first of these, not surprisingly, is the institution that most visibly separates capitalism from its preceding social formations. This is the use of markets as the primary means of organizing the activities of production and of distribution—activities almost exclusively dominated by Tradition for the first ninety-nine percent of human existence, and by Command for most of the remainder, starting perhaps around the third or second millennium B.C. Nonetheless, for all its striking prominence and operational importance, the market is only one of the crucial elements of capitalism and, in my estimation, not that of the greatest significance when it comes to looking into the future.

Far more important for that purpose is the complex entity to which capitalism owes its internal energy and historical momentum, not to mention its name—capital. At the risk of saying what everyone already knows, I must stress that capital is not the same as wealth, which long predates it. The difference is that capital is a dynamic concept and wealth is not. Kings and pharaohs did not build palaces to rent them out, or seek gold to buy mean objects like coal or cloth in the hope of selling them at a profit. As Marx was the first to see, the institution of capital requires a change of perspective that transforms wealth from a thing into a process, in which coal is turned into money which is then used to buy more coal, which in turn will be sold— hopefully, for more money than was needed to buy it. Nothing like such a continuous self-expanding process existed in the precapitalist world of wealth. I need hardly add that under the bland description of "investment spending," this circuit of capital becomes the very life-blood of the capitalist world.

The process of capital accumulation appeared as a commercial class formed within the decaying framework of feudalism, and with it came an immense force for social change. If markets are the key institution by which capitalism escapes the routines of Tradition and the vagaries of Command, that which supplies both the psychological energy and the behavioral predictability that makes markets "work" is the displacement of feudal or imperial political ambitions by those of the mercantile class. The appellation "economic" makes it clear that these ambitions were not aimed at an extension of rulership, which was the main expression of political life before capitalism. But there is no concealing the fact that economic expansion resulted in, even if it did not spring from, an extension of political power, as the mercantile class now began to contend with the older aristocratic order for representation in, and then for direct entry into, the institutions of rulership itself.

This brings to attention a third identifying aspect of capitalism that bears with equal—perhaps even greater—importance on the future of the system. It is the peculiar shape that power itself assumes, once capital accumulation becomes a new form in which it makes itself manifest. This is a bifurcation of power into two coexistent realms. One of these, of ancient heritage, continues the traditional functions of governance, now more and more organized according to liberal political principles, but still largely occupied with the maintenance of law and order within the state, and with foreign relations, including war, with other states. In the newly constituted "economic" realm, however, power assumes a different form and concerns itself with different objectives. It is not directly connected with the promulgation of law and order or the conduct of foreign relations, but with control over production and distribution, and it exercises this power not by "governmental" compulsions and punishments, but by the exercise of disciplinary authority over "its" work forces, above all, the right to fix the terms of employment or to terminate it, and the right to ownership of all output that emerges from its undertakings.

For all the difficulties of drawing a map of these two realms with accuracy, we commonly talk about the coexistence of two intermingled, but distinctive "sectors," one public, the other private. Moreover, this widely recognized division of power is generally perceived as the locus of a major problem with respect to the prospects for capitalism—namely, the necessity for the two realms to cooperate for what political economy would call the successful realization of capital accumulation—what economics calls "growth." It is here, as I am certain Leonard Silk would have agreed, that economics must come to terms with politics and politics with economics—a state of affairs that seems very far from being realized in our country today.

This is not yet the place to describe what "coming to terms" implies with respect to either or both realms. As we can perhaps anticipate, it is very doubtful that it can be described in simple or unchanging terms. The relation of the two realms does, however, admit of clarification by ridding it of conceptions that distort both sides of the issue, all the more so for being unintentional as well as unrecognized. I therefore begin with a seemingly trifling matter that has, I guarantee, anything but trifling consequences.

The matter is the change in our point of view in considering the same problems in the two realms—or more analytically, the mind-set that inclines us to see differences between the public and private sectors, where there are in fact similarities. A few down-to-earth examples will give this general charge a cutting edge.

My first case in point will be the treatment of the term "debt" in the two sectors. By general consensus, the debt of the public sector constitutes a burden on future generations, and as a consequence, a drag on growth. If the debts of private enterprises exercise any such negative influence, we rarely hear about it. From this negative construal of public debts, it follows that the smaller the public debt, the less the burden; and that the optimal state of affairs would be a condition of zero debt. What goes unnoticed in this earnest assertion is that a nation with no public debt must be a nation without Treasury bonds or notes whose distinctive attribute is that they carry the promise of reimbursement at maturity by the government itself.

That statement always brings a reaction of shock. In what securities would a nation without a national debt invest its Social Security Trust Fund? What bonds or notes would the Federal Reserve use for its open market operations, or commercial banks or corporations or private households for the safekeeping of their core reserves?

The shock, of course, comes from the realization that zero national debt would constitute cause for national, perhaps international, alarm, rather than national celebration. But why is this not immediately apparent? Is it not clear that the "debt" of a national government is not the same thing as the debts of private entities? The latter are only as strong as the capability of their issuers to realize the funds needed to redeem them. The former has no such limitation, insofar as national governments create their own money. Of course even national states can go bankrupt and their bonds become so much wallpaper, but to the best of my knowledge this has occurred only when the issuing governments have been defeated in war and thereby lost their sovereign prerogatives, as in the cases of the Confederate States of America and the Czarist government of Russia. Otherwise national debts are always redeemable, although to be sure, the value of the money in which they are paid off will diminish if inflationary forces, perhaps fueled by excessive government spending, race out of control. On the other hand, the same inflationary devaluation can arise from excessive private spending, with the same effects for private bonds.

I trust the purpose of this excursion is apparent. It is to show that the same terms are differently appraised when they refer to the operations of the private and the public sectors. Private corporate debt is not perceived as a burden, but as an asset—sometimes risky, to be sure, but a form of wealth that our children will bless us for leaving to them in our safety deposit boxes. Public debts, never considered as government bonds, are not so pictured. What we have here is a striking example of two problems that interfere with the successful guidance of the economy—first, that the public understanding of government debt is incomplete and seriously distorted, not least by our public representatives themselves; and second, that even economists, whose training should make them agents for public enlightenment, seem on all too many occasions to be enthralled by the same misperceptions as their should-be students.

The consequences of this misperception are so important that I shall continue further by considering the related matter of deficit spending. If debts are regarded with unease, deficits are viewed with genuine fear. On the part of liberals and conservatives alike there is agreement that a balanced budget is an imperative goal of national economic policy within seven or ten years. The most commonly heard reason for this is that some expenditures, mainly in health care, are rising at rates that far outpace any realistic projections of tax revenues, with the consequence that our annual national borrowing—our deficit—threatens to reach "unsustainable" proportions.

Let me begin to examine this argument by noting that the private sector also incurs deficits—that is, borrowing. For 1995 the on-budget government deficit is estimated at around $250 billion, whereas total corporate borrowings are projected at something just under $350 billion. Nonetheless, the first is regarded with trepidation, while the second is viewed with approbation. We shall explore the reasons in a moment, but the very fact that business borrowing is not called "deficitary" is itself an instance of the failure of economics to view the operations of the two sectors through a single lens.

The conventional explanation for this is that private borrowing is used for investment—that is, for purposes whose benefits will be reaped in terms of economic growth, whereas no comparable claim can be made for Treasury borrowing. This does not mean, however, that there is no investment component in federal spending. The problem, rather, is that the volume of private investment spending can be readily ascertained insofar as borrowing for investment purposes is identified as such by firms, whereas there is nothing like a comparable "capital budget" for the borrowing operations of our national government. As a result, one cannot separate federal expenditures for routine operational expenditures from those for investment purposes. Quite correctly, the investment banker Felix Rohatyn has described the federal budget as "a grotesque document that reflects neither accounting nor economic reality."[1]

Is it possible, nonetheless, to ascertain the volume of government borrowing for investment purposes? Some years ago the well-known financial analyst Peter Bernstein and I tried to estimate what a plausible figure might be. We started with a calculation by the Office of Management and Budget that estimated the size of federal investment outlay during the late 1980s to be something over $200 billion per year, which was, in fact, more or less equal to the deficits of those years, although this was not pointed out by the OMB. We reduced this total by about three quarters by ridding it of such items as defense-related expenditures, commodity loans, transfers to state and local governments, and a few other such purposes that the OMB deemed dubious as investments, but which still left enough to yield a quite respectable federal investment total of about $40 billion. This was probably a considerable underestimate. For instance, a considerable portion of federal transfers to state and local governments are used for roads, tunnels, bridges, and education, although these expenditures are not credited to the federal government as investment. In total, these transfers came to $137 billion in 1990 and would probably exceed $200 billion today.[2]

What a careful estimate of total federal investment would amount to today is beyond my powers of computation. Worse, it seems to be mainly beyond the concerns of economic statisticians. The widely known economist William Nordhaus, for example, has complained that our national accounts for "investment" are sorely at variance with what the term is presumed to mean—to wit, expenditures whose returns will increase rather than sustain the existing level of output. "Domestic investment," he writes, referring to the sum of both private and public sectors, "includes only business or quasi-business purchases of long-lived tangible assets—structures, equipment and inventories. It excludes all government investments, all business intangible investments, as well as much activity in the household sector that is of an investment nature."

This means, Nordhaus goes on to point out, that the official figures for investment exclude government road-building (evidently not a "structure"), as well as research, education, and health. Making his own estimates for the categories of investment that escape these arbitrary definitions, Nordhaus more than doubles the estimated rate of national savings whence arises the bulk of national investment, private and public.[3]

I have no doubt that a recognition of the Procrustean nature of our accounting definitions could go a long way to calming the public's anxiety about the deficit problem. But I rather doubt that the accounting changes will be made before there is change in our stubborn tendency to see public financial matters in a different light from private ones. The problem is exemplified in a recent interview with Robert Reischauer, a former director of the Congressional Budget Office and now a senior staff member of the Brookings Institution.[4] Asked whether there was not a parallel between private investment and that portion of the national budget undertaken for capital purposes—roads and bridges as the standard example—Reischauer replies:

> In theory there are several attractive aspects of dividing government spending into capital accounts and operating accounts. But in practice it is difficult to imagine such a system working well. The division of government activities between the capital and operating accounts would not be done in an analytically justifiable way. Politics would enter into the definitions of capital and operating accounts. We would be left with a worse situation than we have now—with pork unfettered by budget constraints.

His interrogator then asks:

> You say that in practice it may be difficult to divide activities between capital and operating accounts, but most of the states do this already.

Reischauer responds:

> Most states use a rather narrow definition of capital that includes only certain types of physical capital. The federal government does not engage in much direct physical capital investment. Most of the physical capital investment made with federal dollars is made by the states for highways, airports, and buildings. The federal government does not own these assets.

The interrogator persists:

> If there were an independent board similar to the Federal Accounting Standards Board, which would define capital narrowly, would this remove the political element?

Reischauer is adamant:

> I doubt it would be possible to protect decisions of such a board from political pressure. But of more importance, a narrow definition of capital, one that covered only physical investment, would bias the decision process because it would miss what are the most important investment activities of the federal government. The federal investments that are most important for strengthening the

long-run potential of the economy are spending on education, training, research and development, child nutrition, and child health.

This is a curious and revealing dialogue. To begin, figures for recent years show a much larger deficit because health expenditures have risen so rapidly. Yet Reischauer himself declares that it is this kind of social restorative spending, not the conventional physical capital, that constitutes the "real" leverage that government makes for our national growth. I have no idea how much pork could be found in our Medicare and health programs, but I should guess that at the least a quarter of our $250–odd billion of health-related expenditure could be safely classified as productivity-related. Quite by itself, this would reduce our "wasteful" deficit to about $160 billion, or a little over 2 percent of GDP, hardly a figure to worry about.[5] And we have not even included the public investment for such purposes as flood control, aviation guidance, health research, education, and the above mentioned state and local investment transfers.

In short, there is an analog to the accumulation of private capital in the accumulation of public capital—an analog unknown to most noneconomists and ignored by all too many economists. There is, to be sure, also a profound difference between the two categories. Private investment, which is capital accumulation in the original sense, aims at returning to its principals the monies they have laid out. Profits can thus be seen as the stream by which expenditures made to achieve private purposes return to those who have risked their assets.

In the public sector a different accounting procedure is perforce in order. There is no way for public expenditures to return directly to the public spending source unless fees are levied for the uses to which the expenditure is put. If every child were charged a high enough tuition for its public school education, every motorist sent a monthly bill for the highway miles on his automatic registering mechanism, every Medicare patient presented with an account of her charges, then federal agencies could justify their programs by comparing costs and returns, and could even make profits, like their private counterparts. The difficulty, of course, is that this would no longer be government, but private enterprise raised to the level of a public disbursement agency. A more traditional view holds that just as the flow of government spending is determined by the advancement of the public weal, with all the imperfections of any democratic process, so its expenses must be borne by the same public, partly by the tax revenues that provide the bulk of government's costs, partly by the borrowing that is an appropriate source for its investment spending.

But what of the pork? Again the curious politics of apolitical economics enters into the determination. It arises when economists speak of the danger that excessive government borrowing will raise interest rates and thereby "crowd out" private investment. The question that is overlooked is whether the net effect of crowding out may not on occasion be beneficial for the nation's economic and social well-being. If, for instance, the rise in interest rates were to make unprofitable the newest Disneyland wonderpark or the flotation of bonds intended to finance another massive takeover, in order to assure the continuance of a program of child vaccination or scientific research, could anyone claim that the country was the loser as a result?

The problem, of course, is that we have no way of easily comparing the respective net social products of the two sectors. Hence my purpose is not to urge obedience to nonexistent or unreliable measurement techniques. It is, rather, to call attention to the fact that the private sector very possibly contains as much social pork as the public sector contains economic pork. The difference is that private pork is justified in terms of its private profits, whereas public pork has no such convenient offset, save the votes it gains its sponsors. But votes do not enter the economists' calculus, whereas profits do. This is why, despite its skirt-lifting, economics is in fact "political," whether or not it recognizes the fact.

A last note on budgets before widening my lens. An approach to economic problems that gave open recognition to the institutional needs of a capitalist social order would not dismiss, or minimize, the "budget" problem. The volume of government expenditures, whether these are financed from taxation or borrowing, is certainly important, although probably not so much as the character of those expenditures, for example, defense, "pork," infrastructure, education, or health. And I have not even mentioned the extremely important consideration of using budget policy to stimulate or to restrain the pace of economic activity. Given the uncertainties that always surround prospective rates of private capital accumulation, one can never declare with any high degree of certainty what the "optimal" levels of government spending would be. Nevertheless, I believe that political economy can make one statement that economics could, but does not make. A society that gains its vitality from the accumulation of private capital will endanger its well-being if it fails to provide for the accumulation of its social capital through the investment operations of its public sector. Like zero debt, zero deficit would be a very dangerous policy to pursue.

Finally I return to a consideration of capitalism as a whole to widen still further our perception of the political aspects of its

economy and its economics. Here I start with a second look at the
market network that is the focus for much economic analysis—
indeed, the sine qua non for its existence. Markets are the institutions that turn the acquisitive drive against itself, as buyers and
sellers are led to take opposing actions in response to identical
stimuli. It is this opposition of behaviors to identical stimuli that
confers upon economics its extraordinary systemic properties,
the envy of all social inquiry.

Is there a political, as well as a strictly economic aspect to this
well-known attribute of markets? I believe there is in the fact
that the outcome of market behavior has two aspects, one much
celebrated by economics, the other noted, but not given its political importance. The aspect that commands the attention of economists is that market outcomes can be described as "utility maximizing" with respect to the actors involved, an outcome for
which no such claims can be made with regard to Tradition- or
Command-oriented orders. The less advertised aspect is that
these same market-determined outcomes also generate "externalities"—that is, utility-lowering consequences. These unwelcome market outcomes range from such public side-effects as the
smoke pollution "bads" that are produced along with "goods,"
to unwanted effects of the production process on the well-being
of producers, a famous case being Adam Smith's warning that
the market-guided division of labor, although very effective in
reducing costs, would make laborers "as stupid and ignorant as
it is possible for a human creature to become."[6]

To be sure, externalities are developed in all social formations—hunting-and-gathering tribes as well as feudal systems
must make whatever efforts they can to avoid the over-exploita-
tion of their lands. What interests us here is that the universality
and importance of the externalities generated in industrial capi-

talism require that its market system be considerably regulated. There is no way of protecting the members of a market society from the pervasive and often dangerous side-effects of their activities except by the imposition of social controls over the market's dispositions—taxes, inducements, prohibitions, or regulations—and there is no source of such protective measures other than recourse to a public sector. All forms of capitalisms, precisely because they depend on the workings of the market, must also depend on political intervention into those workings, although that fact is rarely recognized, and still more rarely, if ever, celebrated.[7]

I pass next to the political element that forms part of the accumulation process. It is obvious that accumulation, like market dynamics, rests on a base of laws that provides the birth certificate of capital itself. But there is a further engagement with politics beyond the protection of private property. As all economists admit, if the process of accumulation is the great constructive process within capitalism, it is also its great deconstructive force. When accumulation falters, the immediate economic consequence is unemployment, insofar as a deceleration of investment typically lessens the need for the existing complement of workers. Does this deceleration also have a political aspect? It assuredly does in that unemployment entails not only a decrease in income payments to those affected, but a deterioration of their social condition. If that deterioration is sufficiently large, it poses a threat not only to the smooth workings of the economy, but to the stability of the government, and perhaps to the socioeconomic order itself. This effect becomes increasingly real as automation brings unemployment into the offices of middle management as well as to the factory floor.

Is the relief of this unemployment to be considered an "economic" or a "political" problem for capitalism? As with market externalities, macro-economic failures are economic insofar as they arise from dysfunctions in the workings of the system, but they are political insofar as their relief requires the action of the public sector, whether this be a change in the quantity of money, the deficit, the level of tariffs, the length of the workday or workweek, and so on. Thus the macro accumulation process imposes social externalities as does the micro production or distribution process, and in both cases the only remedial force is the use of the powers of the public realm.

These arguments lead to what many will consider an unwelcome conclusion. It is that economics is of necessity political. One would think such a conclusion obvious on considering that the institutions of capitalism are not only markets and accumulation, both of which require political intervention for their effective operation, but the bifurcation of political authority itself into two realms, one "private" or "economic"; one "public" or "governmental." This bifurcation does not mean that capitalism is therefore a nonpolitical social formation. It means that it has two sources of the authority without which no stratified social system can exist.

One of these, it is worth repeating, is the continuance of the age-old duties of government, with its tasks of defense and justice and (under capitalism) the provision of social capital.[8] The second realm of power lies in the economy itself—not merely in the property-oriented nature of its very existence, but in its reliance on public intervention to protect the larger formation from malfunctions that have their origins in the workings of the market and the accumulation process. Capitalism is therefore not only political in its origins, as are all social formations, but it remains political in its dependency on "government" to assure its continuing viability.

My peroration is self-evident. The key for capitalism's future lies above all else in the cooperation of the sectors, and this in turn depends on the mutual regard of its social classes on the one hand, and of its public and private leaders and functionaries on the other. When we compare the prospects for variations of capitalism around the world—Swedish, German, French, Korean, or American—it seems to me that the relation of the public and private sectors is, more than any other single factor, the most important variable in determining their respective futures. I hardly need to add that with respect to this crucial need to cultivate a climate of mutual regard between private and public elites, and the even more fundamental necessity for a basic legitimacy to be accorded by the public to the economic functions of government, the United States comes out very poorly.

This feature of low regard is surely grounds for uneasy expectations with regard to capitalism's prospects in the United States. Yet I recall the quite different climate of an earlier time—not only the New Deal Era, but Kennedy and Truman and Johnson's pre-Vietnam War years. That recollection gives me reason to hope that the current mood of mindless anti-governmentalism may not last long. I make so bold as to think that Leonard Silk would have agreed with this conclusion, if not with all of the argument that has preceded it. The question I must put to my professional associates, the economists, is whether they will play a role in this sorely needed transformation of understandings by making their study the political economy of real-world capitalism, not the economics that is only its textbook shadow.

NOTES

....

Notes to Chapter 1

1. Newt Gingrich, remarks at the Washington Research Group Symposium, November 11, 1994, in Ed Gillespie and Bob Schellhas, eds., *Contract with America* (New York: Times Books, 1995), 189.

2. Dick Armey, *The Freedom Revolution* (Washington, D.C.: Regnery, 1995), 19.

3. Werner Stark, *The Contained Economy: An Interpretation of Medieval Economic Thought* (The Papers of the Aquinas Society of London, No. 26, London, 1956). Reprinted in Leonard Silk and Mark Silk, *The Evolution of Capitalism* (New York: Arno Press, 1972), 18–193.

4. Adam Smith, *An Inquiry into the Nature and Causes of the Wealth of Nations* (1776; 5th ed. 1789; reprint New York: Random House, 1937), 13–14.

5. Max Weber, *The Protestant Ethic and the Spirit of Capitalism,* trans. Talcott Parsons (1904; reprint New York: Scribners, 1958).

6. Joseph A. Schumpeter, *Capitalism, Socialism, and Democracy,* 3rd ed. (New York: Harper, 1950), 120–21.

7. Karl Marx and Friedrich Engels, *The Communist Manifesto,* trans. Samuel Moore (1888; reprint Harmondsworth: Penguin, 1967), 85.

8. For a recent version of this point of view, see Armey, *The Freedom Revolution,* 49.

9. Anatoly Dobrynin, *In Confidence* (New York: Times Books, 1995), 611.

10. See Seweryn Bialer, "The Death of Soviet Communism," *Foreign Affairs* 70, no. 5 (Winter 1991–92), 168.

11. Robert G. Kaiser, *Why Gorbachev Happened* (New York: Simon and Schuster, 1992), 77.

12. Dobrynin, *In Confidence,* 636.

13. *Ibid.,* 633.

14. See Philip Hanson, "Soviet Economic Reform: Perestroika or 'Catastroika?' " *World Policy Journal* VIII, no. 2 (Spring 1991), 289–316.

15. Quoted in Kaiser, *Why Gorbachev Happened*, 360.

16. Quoted in Hanson, "Soviet Economic Reform," 306.

Notes to Chapter 2

1. Figures here are taken from *World Economic Survey* (New York: United Nations, 1992), 1.

2. See articles by Zvi Griliches, Dale W. Jorgenson, Mancur Olson, and Michael J. Boskin in "Symposium on the Slowdown in Productivity Growth," *The Journal of Economic Perspectives* (Fall 1988), 9–97; and Martin Neil Baily and Robert J. Gordon, "The Productivity Slowdown, Measurement Issues, and the Explosion of Computer Power," *Brookings Papers on Economic Activity* 2 (1988), 347–431.

3. *Financial Times*, Nov. 17, 1992.

4. Akio Mikuni, "The Collapse in Japanese Financial Markets," Tokyo, September 1992.

5. K. S. Courtis, "Why Japan Will Come Back," *The International Economy* (September-October 1992), 1.

6. Alan Greenspan, remarks at a press conference, American Embassy, Tokyo, Oct. 14, 1992.

7. Alan Greenspan, testimony before the Committee on Banking, Housing, and Urban Affairs, United States Senate, July 21, 1992.

8. See Jeffrey E. Garten, *A Cold Peace: America, Japan, Germany, and the Struggle for Supremacy* (New York: Times Books, 1992).

Notes to Chapter 3

1. Max Weber, *The Protestant Ethic and the Spirit of Capitalism*, trans. Talcott Parsons (1904; reprint New York: Scribners, 1958), 181–82.

2. Newt Gingrich, *To Renew America* (New York: HarperCollins, 1995), 7, 34, 43.

3. For a thorough exposition of this doctrine, see Francis X. Sutton et al., *The American Business Creed* (Cambridge, Mass: Harvard University Press, 1962).

4. This was the view of William Feather, a publishing executive and contributor to *Nation's Business* in the 1920s. Quoted in James W. Pro-

thro, *The Dollar Decade* (Baton Rouge: Louisiana State University Press, 1954), 43.

5. Milton Friedman, *Capitalism and Freedom* (Chicago: University of Chicago Press, 1962), 133.

6. Thomas J. Watson, Jr., interview with Leonard Silk, Armonk, N.Y., February 6, 1965. Quoted in Leonard S. Silk, "The Role of the Business Corporation in the Economy and Society," in Robert S. Smith and Frank T. deVyver, eds., *Economic Systems and Public Policy: Essays in Honor of Calvin Bryce Hoover* (Durham, N.C.: Duke University Press, 1966), 85.

7. See *Who's Minding the Store? The Report of the Twentieth Century Fund Task Force on Market Speculation and Corporate Governance* (New York: Twentieth Century Fund Press, 1992).

8. Interview with Leonard Silk, quoted in Silk, "The Role of the Business Corporation in the Economy and Society," 87.

9. Alexis de Tocqueville, *Democracy in America* (1835; reprint Garden City, N.Y.: Doubleday, 1969), 526.

10. See Jay Fliegelman, "Authorizing the Declaration," *New York Times,* July 4, 1993, E11.

11. For the social welfare version, see John Rawls's *A Theory of Justice* (Cambridge, Mass.: Harvard University Press, 1971). For the libertarian approach, see the work by Rawls's Harvard colleague Robert Nozick, *Anarchy, State, and Utopia* (New York: Basic Books, 1974).

12. Daniel W. Bromley, "Russian Roulette: Plato, Smith, Hamilton, Madison, Marshall, and Marx" (Unpublished paper, University of Wisconsin, 1992).

13. Jonathan R. T. Hughes, *The Governmental Habit Redux* (Princeton, N.J.: Princeton University Press, 1991), 20–53.

14. Lincoln Steffens, *Autobiography* (New York: Harcourt, Brace, Jovanovich, 1958), 196.

15. Hughes, *The Governmental Habit Redux*, 91.

16. Herbert Hoover, campaign speech, Madison Square Garden, October 31, 1932; in William Star Myers, ed., *The State Papers and Other Public Writings of Herbert Hoover,* vol. II (Garden City, N.Y.: Doubleday, Doran, 1934), 428.

17. See Hughes, *The Governmental Habit Redux*, ch. 5.

18. See Leonard Silk, *Nixonomics* (New York: Praeger, 1973).

19. Academics, of whom Michael C. Jensen was the most important, played a major role in providing the rationale for the takeover boom;

see his "Takeovers: folklore and science," *Harvard Business Review* (No-vember-December 1984), 109–21.

20. L. William Seidman, *Full Faith and Credit: The Great S&L Debacle and other Washington Sagas* (New York: Times Books/Random House, 1993).

21. David A. Stockman, *The Triumph of Politics: Why the Reagan Revo-lution Failed* (New York: Harper & Row, 1986), 13.

22. Quoted in Stanley B. Greenberg, *Middle Class Dreams: The Politics and Power of the New American Majority* (New York: Times Books, 1995), 282–83.

23. David Frum, *Dead Right* (New York: Basic Books, 1994), 188.

24. Roger Pilon, "Freedom, Responsibility, and the Constitution: On Recovering Our Founding Principles," in David Boaz and Edward H. Crane, eds., *Market Liberalism: A Paradigm for the 21st Century* (Washing-ton, D.C.: Cato Institution, 1993), 27.

25. Michael Lienesch, *Redeeming America: Piety and Politics in the New Christian Right* (Chapel Hill: University of North Carolina Press, 1993), 120–21.

26. Gingrich, *To Renew America*, 7, 8, 57.

27. Dick Armey, *The Freedom Revolution* (Washington, D.C.: Regnery, 1995), 13.

28. Gingrich, *To Renew America*, 67.

29. Armey, *The Freedom Revolution*, 34, 311.

30. *Ibid.*, 44, 191–92.

Notes to Chapter 4

1. See, for example, Anders Aslund "Eurasia Letter: Ukraine's Turn-around," *Foreign Affairs* (September 22, 1995).

2. See J. Melitz and C. Waysand, "The Role of Government Aid to Firms During the Transition to a Market Economy: Russia 1992–94," Center for Economic Policy Research, September 1994.

3. According to the *Financial Times* (June 27, 1995), "The Russian Federation now has 1.7 times more bureaucrats than the Soviet Union had in 1989, despite there being 130 million fewer people to adminis-ter . . . "

4. *The Economist* (October 7, 1995) reports that of the 70,000 employ-ees of Goskomstat, *six* were engaged in compiling national accounts in the home office.

5. *The Economist*, July 22, 1995.

6. *New York Times*, August 1, 1995.

7. K. P. O'Prey, *A Farewell to Arms: Russia's Struggle with Defense Conversion* (New York: The Twentieth Century Fund Press, 1995), 20.

8. O'Prey, *A Farewell to Arms*, 21.

9. "Reconstruction and Development of the Industrial Sector of Mongolia," The Boston Consulting Group (Boston: November 1992).

10. This conclusion is based on regressions run on World Bank data from the World Development Report of 1993 (Washington, D.C.: World Bank, 1993). Income data are corrected for purchasing power.

11. Melitz and Waysand, "The Role of Government Aid to Firms." This figure illustrates dramatically how little value is added to raw materials by the inherited industrial establishment.

12. Several commentators have attributed the collapse of CMEA trade to the collapse of the payment system: Without an internationally acceptable means of payment, firms in newly separated countries refused to trade. I doubt that the payment regime was the fundamental problem, particularly since intracountry trade suffered greatly too. More important was the fact that the output of most firms could not compete internationally. See Jefferey D. Sachs, "Crossing the Valley of Tears in Eastern Europe," *Challenge* (September-October 1991). See also Richard O'Brien and Ingrid Iverson, "The Roles of Incentives and Planning in Market Oriented Transformations," in *Finance and the International Economy* (New York: Oxford University Press for the AMEX Bank Review, 1992).

13. These figures result from regression analysis of data from the 1993 World Development Report.

14. W. Wasterly, M. de Melo, and G. Ofer, "Services as a Major Source of Growth in Russia and Other Former Soviet States," *Policy Working Paper 1292* (Washington, D.C.: World Bank, April 1994).

15. S. Commander and R. Yemtsov argue that unemployment in Russia has remained quite low—below 6 percent—because "[c]ontrary to Eastern European experience[,] Russian firms have not operated as if governed ex-ante by a hard budget constraint." That is, they have expected subsidies and they have received them. ("Russian Unemployment: Magnitude, Characteristics and Dimensions," *Policy Research Working Paper 1426* [Washington, D.C.: World Bank, February 1995]). Commander and Yemtsov's optimism about the Eastern European experience is tempered by the evidence. Against signs of substantial restruc-

turing (through 1993) in the Czech and Slovak Republics and some restructuring in Poland and Hungary, the record for Bulgaria gives modest reason for optimism and for Romania and the Former Soviet Union, practically none. (B. Hoekman and G. Pohl "Enterprise Restructuring in Eastern Europe: How Much? How Fast? Where?" *Policy Research Paper 1433* [Washington, D.C.: World Bank, March 1995]).

16. Joshua Aizenman and Peter Isard, "Resource Allocation During the Transition to a Market Economy: Policy Implications of Supply Bottlenecks and Adjustment Costs," *Working Paper 4366* (Cambridge, Mass.: National Bureau of Economic Research, May 1993).

17. Michael P. Dooley and Peter Isard, "The Roles of Incentives and Planning in Market Oriented Transformations," in *Finance and the International Economy*.

18. Eric Rice, "Managing the Transition: Enhancing the Efficiency of Eastern European Governments," *Working Paper WPS 757* (Washington, D.C.: World Bank, August 1991).

19. See, for example, M. Boycko, A. Schleifer, and R. W. Vishny, "Privatizing Russia" in *Brookings Papers on Economic Activity 2/1993*, and the discussion that follows.

20. See Kathy Krumm, Branko Milanovic, and Michael Walton, "Transfers and the Transition From Central Planning," *Finance and Development* (September 1995). The title, like the contents of the article and of the World Bank Working Paper on which it is based, pays little attention to the role of state firms in administering the transfer payment system. This role is crucial because part of the pressure to sustain firms stems from their role as providers of public goods and transfers. By focusing on the dangers of excessive transfers and the need to observe budget constraints, the article characteristically neglects the institutional reforms that must accompany stabilization if it is to work.

Notes to Chapter 5

1. For estimates on China's growth rate, see Dwight Perkins, "Completing China's Move to the Market," *Journal of Economic Perspectives* 8, 2 (Spring 1994), 24–25; and Robert Mundell, "Is China's Supergrowth Sustainable?" *The International Economy* (July-August 1995), 20.

2. Directorate of Intelligence, Central Intelligence Agency, "The Chi-

nese Economy in 1991 and 1992: Pressure to Revisit Reform Mounts" (August 1992), 11.

3. *Wall Street Journal*, May 24, 1994.

4. Gary H. Jefferson and Thomas G. Rawski, "Enterprise Reform in Chinese Industry," *Journal of Economic Perspectives* 8, no. 2 (Spring 1994), 64.

5. Cited in Perry Link, "The Old Man's New China," *The New York Review of Books* (June 9, 1994), 32–33.

6. Uli Schmetzer, "Life in the New China," *The Brown Journal of World Affairs*, II, no. 1 (Winter 1994), 165.

7. Policy Impact Panel on the Future of U.S.-China Relations, Council on Foreign Relations, Release dated May 11, 1994.

8. *The Brown Journal of World Affairs*, II, no. 1 (Winter 1994), 169–73.

Notes to Chapter 6

1. Quoted in *Wall Street Journal*, June 8, 1993. See also Bob Davis, "Clinton's Get-Tough Stance With Japan Signals Rise of Revisionist Thought," *Wall Street Journal*, June 14, 1993.

2. Chalmers Johnson, "Capitalism: East Asian Style," The 1992 Panglaykim Memorial Lecture (Jakarta, December 15, 1992).

3. See, for example, Eamonn Fingleton, "Japan's Invisible Leviathan," *Foreign Affairs* (March-April, 1995), 69–85.

4. *Cleveland Plain Dealer*, July 13, 1993.

5. See Peter F. Drucker, "The End of Japan, Inc.? An Economic Monolith Fractures," *Foreign Affairs* (Spring 1993).

6. Capital goods—a statistical category that includes manufacturing machinery and components—jumped from 43 percent of Japan's exports in 1981 to 58 percent in 1993. During the same period, the proportion of exports accounted for by consumer durables like cars, stereos, and washing machines dropped from 28 percent to 22 percent. *New York Times*, October 23, 1994.

Notes to Chapter 7

1. Dick Armey, *The Freedom Revolution* (Washington, D.C.: Regnery, 1995), 59.

2. The term "social market economy" was coined by German Christian Democrats in the immediate postwar period to convey their ambition to strike a balance between social protection and market competition. Among political scientists, the countries treated here are often labelled "corporatist." I prefer "social market economy" because its connotations are broader, and more substantive. (The term "corporatism" emphasizes government policy and formal policy-making arrangements.) Though my terminology is different, my conceptualization of the Northern European countries as a distinct constellation of advanced capitalist economies draws heavily on Peter Katzenstein, *Small States in World Markets* (Ithaca: Cornell University Press, 1985), and *Policy and Politics in West Germany* (Philadelphia: Temple University Press, 1987). My approach is also deeply indebted to the work of David Soskice and Wolfgang Streeck. It should be noted that there are important cross-national variations within both the social welfare and free market categories, and that there are many countries, most notably Japan and France, that do not fit easily into either category.

3. Union density and coverage rates are from OECD, *Employment Outlook* (Paris, July 1994), ch. 5.

4. The exception is minimum-wage legislation, which has played a relatively unimportant role in the social market economies for the simply reason that virtually all wages are determined by collective bargaining.

5. See Gösta Esping-Andersen, *The Three Worlds of Welfare Capitalism* (Princeton: Princeton University Press, 1990).

6. OECD, *Employment Outlook* (Paris, July 1993), ch. 5. For further discussion of the differences between the Swedish and German model variants, see Pontusson, "Between Neoliberalism and the German Model: Swedish Capitalism in Transition," in Colin Crouch and Wolfgang Streeck, eds., *Modern Capitalism or Modern Capitalisms?* (London: Francis Pintner, forthcoming).

7. For a concise review of this literature, see Peter Hall, "Central Bank Independence and Coordinated Wage Bargaining," *German Politics and Society* 31 (Spring 1994).

8. See Wolfgang Streeck, "On the Institutional Conditions of Diversified Quality Production" in Egon Matzner and Wolfgang Streeck, eds., *Beyond Keynesianism* (Aldershot: Edward Elgar, 1991).

9. Katzenstein, *Small States in World Markets*.

10. David Goodhart, *The Reshaping of the German Social Market* (London: Institute for Public Policy Research, 1994), 20.

11. OECD, *Historical Statistics 1960–1993* (Paris, 1993).

12. See Paul Pierson, *Dismantling the Welfare State?* (Cambridge: Cambridge University Press, 1994), and "The New Politics of the Welfare State," *World Politics* (forthcoming).

13. See OECD, *Employment Outlook* (Paris, July 1993), ch. 5.

14. All figures in this section are taken from OECD, *Historical Statistics 1960–1993* (Paris, 1993). My discussion of the effects of internationalization has been greatly influenced by the work of Geoffrey Garrett, most notably "Capital Mobility, Trade, and the Domestic Politics of Economic Policy," *International Organization* 49, no. 4 (Autumn 1995).

15. It should be noted that Keynesian deficit spending has never been a distinctive feature of the social market economies; quite the contrary, these countries tended to pursue more restrictive fiscal policies than France, Britain, and the United States in the postwar era.

16. Jonas Pontusson, "Explaining the Decline of European Social Democracy: The Role of Structural Economic Change," *World Politics* 47, no. 4 (1995), 495–533.

Notes to Chapter 8

1. Dick Armey, *The Freedom Revolution* (Washington: Regnery, 1995), 294.

2. Memorandum for Directors and Chiefs of War Department General and Special Division and Bureaus and the Commanding Generals of the Major Commands from General Eisenhower, April 27, 1946, quoted in Seymour Melman, *Pentagon Capitalism, The Political Economy of War* (New York: McGraw-Hill, 1979), Appendix A, 231–34.

3. U.S. State Department Bulletin, vol. 44 (February 6, 1961).

4. Dwight D. Eisenhower, letter to Everett E. Hazlett, *The New York Times*, March 17, 1985, op-ed page.

5. Murray L. Weidenbaum, *Proceedings of the American Economic Association* (December 1987).

6. Herbert Scoville, *MX: Prescription for Disaster* (Cambridge, Mass.: MIT Press, 1981), 56–57.

7. These and subsequent figures are taken largely from the U.S.

Arms Control and Disarmament Agency, *World Military Expenditures and Arms Transfers 1993–1994* (Washington, D.C.: February 1995).

8. Ethan B. Kapstein, "America's Arms-Trade Monopoly," *Foreign Affairs* 73, 3 (May-June 1994), 20–27.

9. *Newsweek*, April 22, 1991, 19.

10. Jeffrey R. Gerlach, "A Post-Cold War Military Budget," in David Boaz and Edward H. Crane, eds., *Market Liberalism: A Paradigm for the 21st Century* (Washington, D.C.: Cato Institute, 1993), 284.

11. Newt Gingrich, *To Renew America* (New York: HarperCollins, 1995), 186–87.

12. *Atlanta Journal-Constitution*, October 15, 1995; October 17, 1995.

13. Ed Gillespie and Bob Schellhas, eds., *Contract With America* (New York: Times Books, 1995), 107.

14. *Economist* (June 4–10, 1994), 18.

15. Ian Anthony, et al., "Arms Production and Arms Trade," *SIPRI Yearbook* (Oxford: Oxford University Press, 1994), 493.

Notes to Chapter 9

1. Newt Gingrich, *To Renew America* (New York: HarperCollins, 1995), 8.

2. Dick Armey, *The Freedom Revolution* (Washington: Regnery Publishing, 1995), 69, 68.

3. Quoted in Michael Lienesch, *Redeeming America: Piety and Politics in the New Christian Right* (Chapel Hill, N.C.: University of North Carolina Press, 1993), 109.

4. See Irving Kristol, "The Cultural Revolution and the Capitalist Future" (1992), in *Neoconservatism: The Autobiography of an Idea* (New York: The Free Press, 1995), 127–28. Kristol, who regularly encourages business folk to feel good about themselves in his contributions to the *Wall Street Journal*'s editorial page, also criticizes Smith for disrespecting the capitalist entrepreneur as "a scheming, conniving, self-seeking, soulless person, always looking for ways to conspire with other businessmen to defeat the workings of the free market and thereby to make illegitimate profits." Almost nowhere in *The Wealth of Nations*, Kristol laments, does the "upright, honest, public-spirited bourgeois businessman make an appearance." Kristol, "Adam Smith and the Spirit of Capitalism" (1976), in *Neoconservatism*, 283.

5. There is good evidence that developing countries that take steps to decrease economic inequality experience stronger growth. See Carl Tham and Dag Ehrenpreis, "The Role of the State and Market in Addressing Inequality and Growth," in Üner Kirdar and Leonard Silk, eds., *A World Fit For People: From Impoverishment to Empowerment* (New York: New York University Press, 1995), 75–86.

6. Douglass C. North, "Economic Performance through Time," Prize Lecture in Economic Science in Memory of Alfred Nobel, Stockholm, December 9, 1993.

7. See Kenneth E. Boulding, *The Structure of a Modern Economy* (New York: New York University Press, 1993), 70–83.

8. See Lawrence Mishel and Jared Bernstein, *The State of Working America, 1994–95* (Washington, D.C.: Economic Policy Institute, 1994), 107–99.

9. Albert Hirschman, *Exit, Voice, and Loyalty: Responses to Decline in Firms, Organizations, and States* (Cambridge, Mass.: Harvard University Press, 1970), 16–17. Friedman's statement can be found in *Capitalism and Freedom* (Chicago: University of Chicago Press, 1962), 91.

10. Armey, *The Freedom Revolution*, 314.

Notes to the Epilogue

1. Felix Rohatyn, "The Budget: Whom Can You Trust?" *New York Review of Books*, August 10, 1995, 49. I shall ignore for simplicity's sake the additional complication of "on-budget" and "off-budget" expenditures—the latter including the Social Security Trust Fund which actually turns the current "off-budget" account from deficit to surplus, although this will not last forever. All my figures concern the deficitary budget.

2. Robert Heilbroner and Peter Bernstein, *The Debt and the Deficit* (New York: W. W. Norton, 1989), 82–89.

3. William D. Nordhaus, "The Federal Budget and National Saving Once Again?" Remarks prepared for the Annual Meeting of the National Association of Business Economists, San Francisco, California, September 11, 1995, 2, 3.

4. Robert Reischauer, quoted in The Jerome Levy Institute, "The Levy Report," Bard College, August 1995, 8.

5. See James K. Galbraith and William Darrity, Jr., "A Guide to the Deficit," *Challenge* (July-August, 1995), 5–12. See also Alex N. McLeod, "The Problem is Inflation-control, not Spending-control," Banco Nazionale Lavoro (Rome), *Quarterly Review* (June 1995): 145–58.

6. Adam Smith, *An Inquiry into the Nature and Causes of the Wealth of Nations* (1776; 5th ed. 1789; reprint New York: Random House, 1937), 734.

7. I consign to a footnote a major problem regarding the market mechanism for which I am unable to come to any trustworthy conclusion. It concerns the rapidly growing presence of a world economy—a geographic entity without definite shape, with many economic centers but no political center, composed of national entities whose economic independence is increasingly exposed to the erosion of transnational market forces. What remains to be seen is the extent to which this new world-straddling aspect of capitalism will also erode the ability of its members to cope with externalities that affect political entities other than those in which they arise—global warming or immigration pressures as cases in point. These effects of "globalization" would seem to require transnational redress which lies as far beyond the grasp of political economy as beyond that of economics.

8. Adam Smith said that the functions of government were three: (1) the defense of the nation from foreign threats; (2) the provision of law, order, and justice; and (3) "that of erecting and maintaining those public institutions and those public works, which, though they may be in the highest degree advantageous to a great society, are, however, of such a nature, that the profit could never repay the expense to any individual or small number of individuals . . . " *Wealth of Nations, 681.*

INDEX